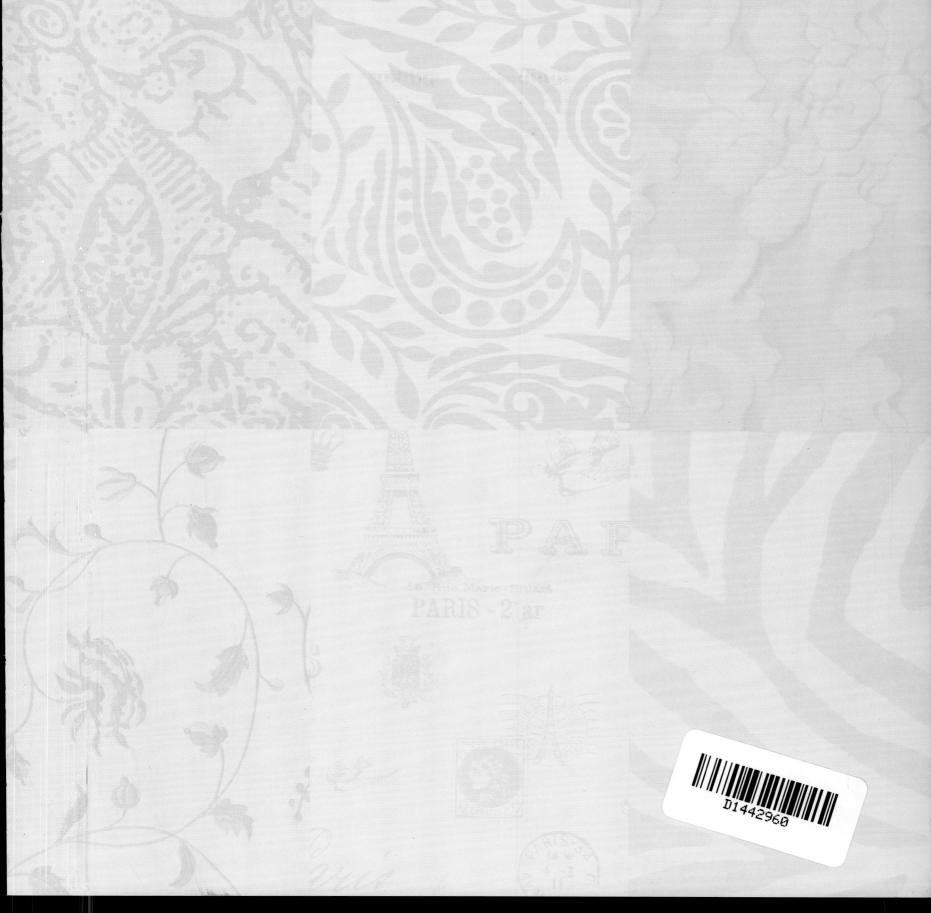

The World in Your Teacup

Written and Produced by

Lisa Boalt Richardson

with

Lauren Rubinstein
Photographer and Food Stylist

Annette Joseph
Coproducer, Art Director,
and Food and Prop Stylist

HARVEST HOUSE PUBLISHERS

EUGENE, OREGON

The World in Your Teacup

Text Copyright © 2010 by Lisa Boalt Richardson
Photography Copyright © 2010 by Lauren Rubinstein

Produced by Lisa Richardson
Photography produced/styled by Annette Joseph

Published by Harvest House Publishers
Eugene, Oregon 97402
www.harvesthousepublishers.com

ISBN 978-0-7369-2580-8

For more information about Lisa Boalt Richardson and tea, go to www.lisaknowstea.com.

Original photography by Lauren Rubinstein. If you are interested in the photos in this book, you may contact Lauren at www.larphotography.com.

Design and production by Garborg Design Works, Savage, Minnesota

Back cover photo of Lisa Richardson by Diane McNamee

Printed in China

10 11 12 13 14 15 16 / NG / 10 9 8 7 6 5 4 3 2 1

This book is dedicated to my loving husband,

JOE RICHARDSON,

a loyal partner in life, parenting, and business.

I look forward to sharing "teatime" with you for

many years to come!

Contents

TYPES OF TEAS

All teas come from the same plant, the Camellia sinensis. The specific types of tea are made by processing the tea leaves differently.

White Tea

Usually just plucked and dried, white tea is the least processed type of tea. Although white tea might contain only the bud of the tea leaf, it may also contain the full leaf. The flavor is delicate, light, and sweet. This type of tea comes mainly from China, but other countries have started to make it as the demand has increased.

Green Tea

To make green teas, the tea leaves are plucked and allowed to wither slightly. They are then quickly processed. In China the leaves are fired in a wok to stop the oxidation. Other countries steam the leaves. The flavor is vegetal and fresh. China, Japan, and Korea are the most famous for making green teas, but other countries make this type as well.

Oolong Tea

These teas can vary from lightly oxidized (more green) to more oxidized (more brown). This is the most "fussy" tea to make and a tea master can really show his expertise with these teas. The flavor range is diverse and can vary from a light and floral (more green) to mellow, sweet, and smooth (more brown). These tea leaves typically lend themselves to more than one steeping. The most famous oolong teas come mainly from China and Taiwan.

Black Tea

Black tea is allowed to fully oxidize; thus, giving it its dark color. In China this tea is sometimes referred to as "red tea." The flavor is well-rounded with a sweet finish. Some have a smoky flavor to them as well. This type of tea is grown and processed around the world.

Puerh Tea

This tea has not been totally dried but is allowed to "ferment" slowly using natural methods, which is known as *sheng* (raw) puerh, or is speeded up through a processing method known as *shou* (ripe or cooked) puerh. The naturally aged teas (*sheng*) can be quite pricey and are the only teas that get better with age. The flavors can vary from fresh and/or earthy to a more delicate and smooth flavor as the tea ages. At this time, puerh tea comes exclusively from China.

Introduction

Ever since I began learning and studying tea, the worldwide importance of this beverage has fascinated me. But as an American and prior to learning about tea in depth, it never occurred to me that a single beverage had such an impact in other countries. On one particular night, after I had studied and read quite a bit about tea traditions, I clearly realized how one beverage can unite people.

My son was in the hospital recovering from mouth surgery. When we moved him from the intensive care unit to a regular hospital room, we met the night nurse who was assigned to his room. Her name was Shirley. After talking to her about the various concerns I had, I asked about her accent and where she was from. When Shirley told me she was from Kenya, I asked if she had lived near the area where the tea plantations were. Then my son piped up and tried to explain to the nurse, as best he could with his very swollen tongue, that I was—as he likes to call me—a "tea lady." When I asked Shirley if she liked tea, her eyes immediately lit up. She told me that my questions reminded her of her home and the wonderful memories of family and friends drinking tea. She smiled and said that because of her and a few others the hospital started serving tea in the cafeteria.

As Shirley tended to my son's medical needs, we talked for more than 45 minutes about our love of tea and the traditions of her native country. She left us for a time and then came back to introduce me to another nurse from Malawi whose father grew tea in that country. We chatted more about tea, and they reminisced about their homelands, tea, and the families they left behind.

It then dawned on me that here are three women, all from different countries, who have been united because of their love of tea. We might not have had anything else in common, but we experienced a bond by sharing our thoughts on that single beverage.

With that as my inspiration, I began to research the bond tea has created between the people of many nations, including my own. I found it fascinating to learn about how the very same beverage became so important to each country and how the practices and ceremonies surrounding that one beverage

differed from one culture to another.

In many parts of the world, drinking tea is an important part of each day and an expression of hospitality. Most of the teatime recipes in this book have been inspired by those who have either lived in the specific country or have enjoyed an extensive visit. The homey recipes include foods that could make up a typical meal or snack commonly served in the homes of those living in that part of the globe. By providing these recipes, I hope you will be able to easily recreate a country's teatime as if you lived there and were inviting guests over to your home. Simply focus on gathering around the table and sharing time with your family and friends over an inviting cup of tea.

I hope you enjoy your travels through this book as you discover tea from around the globe. My daughter likes to say that her favorite place to be is at home reading a book because her imagination can take her anywhere. This trip will only cost you the price of the book and a few ingredients. If the lack of time and money have kept you from traveling, let the countries come to your home as you celebrate with tea from around the world.

China

So often these days, we see "Made in China" printed on the stickers that are stuck to the bottom of items we've purchased. It seems as though it is hard to find anything that is *not* made in China. This was also the case for tea for thousands of years because China not only discovered tea but also held a tight monopoly on it. As the second most popular beverage in the world (water is the first), tea has China to thank for its fame. Whether you like your tea hot or cold, white, green, oolong, black, or puerh—or all of them hot *and* cold as I do—you have China to thank for your drinking pleasure.

TEA PAST

Many legends about how tea was first discovered are in circulation, but there is no debate that China was the country where the entire tea craze got started. One legend states that around 2737 BC, Chinese Emperor Shen Nung was the first person to drink the steaming brew. The story explains that while he was boiling water for drinking, a few tea leaves from a wild tea tree blew into his pot. Whether this is true or simply a myth, what is certain is that all tea originated from China, and its influence has expanded worldwide.

China's history is divided into dynasties. Each dynasty has its own influence, style, and significance to tea history. By the Han Dynasty (206 BC to 220 AD), tea was clearly a significant part of the Chinese empire. Roads were being built so that tea could be transported out of and enjoyed beyond the growing regions. During this period, tea was pressed into a cake form and had a rather bitter taste. It was viewed more as a medicine to help relieve ailments than for drinking pleasure. This attitude occurred well before the discovery of tea's health benefits. I guess the

Chinese really did know a thing or two before the rest of us.

Tea lovers must be grateful to those who made tea taste so wonderful. The process that was developed over thousands of years makes what is poured into our teacups today so pleasurable to drink. During the Feudal Dynasty (220 AD to 618 AD), the Chinese figured out that steaming the tea leaves rids tea of its bitter taste, and tea grew in popularity.

During the Tang Dynasty (618 AD to 906 AD), tea was starting to be considered a beverage that could provide the body with a sense of well-being and overall enjoyment. Also during this time, tea etiquette came into fashion. In his book *Ch'a Ching*, known in English as *The Book of Tea*, which is still in print today, author Lu Yu clearly described a method to cultivate and process tea. However, more than a manual for cultivating tea, this book gave etiquette a new name. Listing 25 utensils that were needed to prepare and serve tea, Lu Yu's tea protocol might have even made etiquette guru Emily Post a little nervous.

Each dynasty made its own unique contribution to the evolution of tea, and the Song Dynasty (960 to 1279) was no different. During this period, different forms of tea were developed. In addition to the traditional pressed cake form, a powdered tea, which was whipped with water, was developed (the Japanese still make matcha tea in this way). The first loose leaf teas were also developed at this time. Although easier to prepare than the cake type, the flavor of the loose leaf tea was bitter and needed refining.

In the Yaun Dynasty (1280 to 1368), a major revelation in the tea industry occurred. The process of "chaoqing," which literally means "roasting out of the green," was discovered. Still in use today, this process consists of hand pressing the withered tea leaves along the sides of a hot wok, giving whole leaf teas, with their various shapes, a beautiful look. But more importantly, this process gives the teas their distinctive Chinese flavor. Chinese teas are famous for their different shapes, and the names of the teas reflect the pride the Chinese take in this process.

To accommodate the loose leaf teas and their enhanced flavors, brewing vessels began to become more and more important. During the Ming Dynasty (1368 to 1644), the *Yixing** teapot was created. These pots were used during the Chinese tea ceremony called *gongfu**, also started during this period and still practiced today.

Yixing teapots are small unglazed clay pots and are considered the best vessels for brewing oolongs. Because they are unglazed, the clay absorbs the flavor of the tea every time tea is brewed. Although this enhances the flavor of the tea, it becomes essential that only one type of tea is used in that particular teapot.

While I am far from an expert in *gongfu*, I have watched the ceremony many times and have enjoyed partaking in it on occasion. The tea is steeped many times, and each infusion brings a new taste. The word *gongfu* means "skill from practice" or "patient effort" and can apply to mastering any art form, including martial arts. Maybe the term "save the best for last" was developed after a Chinese tea ceremony because some fine oolongs can be steeped up to seven times—each infusion tasting better than the last! To learn more about China's *gongfu* tea ceremony, please see the resource guide in the back of this book.

A brewing vessel called a *gaiwan** was another invention that came into use during this time period. A *gaiwan* was developed originally to steep green teas but can also be used to steep all types of tea. It is essentially a teacup with no handle, a lid, and a saucer. Teas can be brewed in a single serving using the *gaiwan*, and more water can be added until the leaves release no more flavor. The lid is used to stir the tea and keep the leaves from escaping while sipping the brew.

The invention of steeping vessels was not the only important contribution during this period in tea's history. Western cultures considered black tea the most significant invention. The industrious Chinese needed to make a tea that was easier to transport over long trade routes and could hold up to harsh conditions. They learned that tea became more travel friendly by allowing it to oxidize longer. The Chinese didn't like this tea (they called it red tea), but they liked the trade value that it brought in addition to the green teas.

The popularity of tea exploded and spread throughout the world during the Qing Dynasty (1644 to 1911). The Chinese profited from this great natural resource by making better tea for transport and by expanding their trade routes. It was during this time that tea finally reached Europe and America.

This relaxing beverage, which so many of us find enjoyable, has had a troubled and turbulent past. Tea's processing secrets have been strictly guarded, and tales of espionage, covert operations, and intrigue swirled around them. Wars have even been fought over tea. All of this, just so countless people could enjoy their coveted cup of tea!

Though today many nations make their own special mark on tea, the Chinese, who developed the processing procedures, gave tea its great taste. They guarded this procedure fiercely because it provided a great source of income. The love for tea has expanded all over the world, but that love has its roots in China.

TEA PRESENT

Because tea has been a part of China's history for so long, tea drinking is to this country as wine drinking may be to the Western culture. It is more than just a beverage. It has symbolism and meaning that goes deeper than quenching one's thirst. Tea represents respect, creates relationships by bringing people together, and is part of a healthy lifestyle. Tea has been a mainstay of religious practices and tea ceremonies for centuries. Although Chinese youth are starting to embrace Western culture, depicted by drinking coffee, tea is still an important part of the society.

China is a large country with many tea traditions. The Chinese tend to not travel long distances, and this has kept each area's tea tradition alive and very much regionalized. In general, the northern part of the country tends to drink jasmine tea from a *gaiwan*. This may be the case in the city of Chengdu, but outside the city, typically a clear glass is used, and green tea is the tea of choice. In the coastal eastern province of Guangdong, they prefer oolong or puerh steeped in small clay teapots.

There are many teahouses all over the country. Originally opened to serve thirsty travelers, teahouses have evolved into meeting places that serve food and provide space to play mahjong or chess, read, or just chat with friends. Some teahouses in the bigger cities have been built as tourist attractions. It is interesting to note that many Chinese carry their own personal brewing devices wherever they go. It may be as fancy as a glass tea brewer or as simple as a handmade bowl, but it is a never-leave-home-without-it device.

Along with the *gongfu* tea ceremony, the Chinese embrace another type of ceremony—the wedding tea ceremony. It is performed by the bride and groom to show respect to their parents and to their heritage. On the morning of the wedding day, the bride serves tea to her parents in their home as a way to thank them for raising her. Depending on personal preferences, a tea ceremony for the groom's family is performed on either the day of the wedding or the day after. In this tradition, together the newlyweds serve tea to the groom's

parents and relatives, sometimes kneeling in front of them. In return for this gesture, the couple receives "lucky red envelopes" full of money or jewelry!

During the Qing Dynasty, the Chinese began using an interesting gesture while tea was being served, and it is still observed today, especially in southern China. If you are unfamiliar with it, you might wonder what all the tapping is about. Legend states that an emperor of the Qing Dynasty liked to travel incognito with his companions throughout the region to "see how the regular people lived" and have

tea with them. As was the custom, each person at the table took a turn pouring tea for the group. When the disguised emperor took his turn, his companions felt compelled to *kowtow* or bow down to show respect to the emperor for his act of kindness. But doing so would have given away the emperor's true identity. Thus, they came up with a way to thank their emperor with a "finger kowtow," better known today as "tea tapping." As tea is being poured, the guest taps two or three fingers on the table three times to show gratitude to the server.

MAKING TEA CHINESE STYLE

The Chinese enjoy so many different types and styles of teas that narrowing them down to one is very difficult. Whichever way you choose to brew your tea, remember that to the Chinese people, drinking tea is all about building relationships.

It can be as simple as placing tea leaves in a heat resistant, single-serving glass container and pouring hot water over the leaves. The Chinese love to watch "the agony of the leaf." As hot water is poured over the leaves, they "agonize" and "dance," floating up and down in the water as they unfurl. Water can be poured over the tea leaves until the flavor has been exhausted. The Chinese tend to drink their teas "straight up," meaning they don't add sugar or milk.

Using a *gaiwan* is another way to steep tea. Select and place a large pinch of tea leaves in the *gaiwan*. Rinse the leaves by pouring the boiling or hot water (depending on type of tea) over the leaves and then quickly drain the water by using the lid to keep the leaves in. Be sure to lift the lid and smell the wonderful aroma of the freshly wet leaves before continuing. Add boiling or hot water a second time by pouring it along the outer side of the cup. This creates some movement of the leaves and helps them infuse properly. Put the lid on top of the cup and allow the tea to steep according to which type of tea—one minute for oolong, two to three minutes for green tea, and three to four minutes for black tea. To drink the tea, lift all three pieces together in one hand, allowing them to rest comfortably in the palm of the dominant hand. Use the thumb to keep them from tilting. Lift the lid with the other hand and tilt just enough to drink from but still closed enough to keep the leaves back. Add fresh hot water to the cup before finishing the first

infusion. Keep adding water until the leaves have lost their flavor.

To make tea *gongfu* style, use a *Yixing* teapot, a waterproof tray* or a tray with drainage holes, and small thimble teacups*. The best tea to use for this is an oolong tea or a puerh tea. Remember to use only one type of tea for each *Yixing* pot because the flavor soaks into the clay. Rinse the teacups and teapot with boiling water. To make a very strong tea concentrate, fill the teapot halfway to two-thirds of the way full with tea leaves, pour hot water over the leaves, and then quickly discard the liquid (this rinses the leaves). Refill the teapot with hot water and allow the leaves to steep a minute or so. The tea is now ready to be poured into the cups. Water may be added to the teapot to steep the tea leaves several more times, allowing a little extra time for each infusion.

Teatime in China

Tea is served from morning until night in China. It is usually served with all meals and in between meals as well. In southern China near the Guangdong area, *dim sum*—sometimes called *yum cha*, which literally means "drink tea"—is very popular. It is a brunch type of meal where many bite-sized dishes are served from trolley carts that servers roll alongside the table.

The circle is a significant shape to the Chinese. It represents wholeness and completeness. Tables in China are almost always round and have a large lazy Susan in the center. If *dim sum* isn't being served on a trolley cart, large platters of food are placed on the lazy Susan, and the meal is served family style. Sometimes diners eat right off the platter with chopsticks and don't have a plate to eat off of at all. Because Chinese manners differ from those in the states, don't be alarmed by the occasional belch. It voices one's satisfaction with the meal.

All of the recipes for this chapter are from Jean Christen, my friend and editor at Harvest House Publishers. Jean was born in China and lived there until she was five years old. Her dad is from the northern area of Xian Province, and her mom is from the Guangdong Province in southern China. These recipes represent a nice mix of the regions. Make your favorite pot of Chinese tea to go with these great recipes, and although fortune cookies have their roots in American culture, add them to the meal for a simple and fun dessert.

RECIPES

Green Onion Crepes

Jean loves these! Her northern dad made these a little thicker and larger and cut and served them like pizza slices, while her southern mom would make them smaller and thinner and served them like thin crepes. Either way, they are delicious!

> 2 cups all-purpose flour
> ½ teaspoon salt
> 1 tablespoon vegetable oil
> 1 cup boiling water
> 3 tablespoons roasted sesame oil
> 3 green onions (green parts only), finely chopped (add
>   more if you love a strong green onion flavor
> oil for frying
> Optional dipping sauce: add a splash of sesame seed oil
>   and a pinch of sugar (or more depending on
>   personal taste) to soy sauce

Mix flour and salt and then add vegetable oil. Slowly add enough boiling water to make dough and stir together with a spoon. When the temperature of the dough has cooled, put dough on a floured surface, knead the dough for 5 minutes or until it's smooth and stretchy (if it's still sticky, add more flour). Cover dough and let it rest for 20 minutes. Then roll the dough into a long roll and pinch off 24 pieces. Put sesame oil in a small bowl. Roll each piece into a flat 4-inch circle and brush generously with sesame oil. Sprinkle ½ to ¾ of the surface with green onions. Roll the closest edge away from you to create a mini log and pinch along the edge to seal in the green onions. Then rotate it 90 degrees and roll log into the shape of a pinwheel. Lay the pinwheel so that its swirls are facing upward and gently roll out the pinwheel into a 4-inch circle. This allows the green onions to be evenly dispersed throughout the pancake. Place each circle on a floured surface or between nonstick paper such as parchment or wax paper. Allow the circles to rest for 10 to 15 minutes. Place a frying pan on burner set to medium to medium high heat and add 1 tablespoon of oil at a time to cook the crepes until they are lightly golden, crispy, and the smell of green onions permeates the air. Remove from pan and set on a paper towel to soak up excess oil. Crepes are best served hot with dipping sauce. To reheat, wrap crepes in foil and place in a 375 degree oven for 10 minutes. Makes 2 dozen.

Fragrant Tea Speckled Eggs

Jean loves to eat these for breakfast, as a high protein savory snack, or as a picnic item. They are beautiful! Most often her mother would toss in several pieces of savory-flavored tofu (dried bean curd). Jean's mom likes to serve chrysanthemum tea with this dish—Jean prefers jasmine tea.

> 3 tablespoons soy sauce (may substitute light soy sauce or Bragg Liquid Aminos)
> 3 tablespoons rice wine
> 1 star anise
> 1 tablespoon granulated sugar
> 1 cinnamon stick
> 3 ¼-inch slice fresh ginger (delete or add more depending on taste)
> 3 tablespoons fragrant dried tea leaves (choose a darker tea that smells good)
> 8 to 12 chicken and/or quail eggs, unpeeled and hard-boiled

Gently roll each hard-boiled egg until shell has a crackled appearance. Set eggs aside. Combine all ingredients (except eggs) in a large kettle. Add 4 cups water and bring to a gentle boil. Reduce heat and simmer for 15 to 20 minutes. Place the eggs into the sauce and continue simmering for 45 minutes. Remove from heat. When cool, carefully take the eggs out of the sauce. Peel, slice, and serve the eggs with sauce ladled over the top of them for additional flavor.

Siu Mai

Many people will recognize this recipe as the quintessential dim sum dish.

> 6 ounces shrimp or prawns, deveined, cleaned, patted dry, and chopped
> ½ cup canned water chestnuts, chopped
> ¼ cup carrots, finely chopped (optional)
> 1 pound ground pork, turkey, or chicken (if using ground turkey or chicken, add 1 tablespoon oil)
> 2 tablespoons soy sauce (may substitute light soy sauce or Bragg Liquid Aminos)
> 1½ tablespoons rice wine
> 2 teaspoons roasted sesame oil
> ¼ teaspoon black pepper, freshly ground
> 2 tablespoons fresh ginger, peeled and finely chopped
> 1 green onion (green part only), finely chopped
> 1 egg white, lightly beaten
> 2 tablespoons cornstarch
> 3 dozen round wonton wraps

Combine all ingredients except wonton wraps. Mix well. To shape *siu mai*, I like to lay the wonton wrapper in my left hand (switch if you are left handed) and place 1 teaspoon mixture in the middle of a wonton. Then with your right hand, dip a finger in some water and rub all around the edges. This will help seal the wrapper closed. Next, carefully squeeze the wonton to create a waist. The shape should look like little drawstring purses. Optional, sprinkle it with a pinch of chopped carrot for color. Line steamers with aluminum foil, nonstick paper, or even Chinese cabbage. Arrange the dumplings in the steamer about ½ inch apart and steam for 15 to 20 minutes. Remove from steamer and serve immediately. If desired, use soy sauce as a dipping sauce. Makes 3 dozen.

England

Although tea made its debut in England in the mid seventeenth century, several factors greatly delayed it from becoming the popular beverage the Brits enjoy today. First sold in coffee houses, tea at one time or another was heavily taxed, illegally smuggled, altered and tainted, fought over, danced around, and sipped by kings and queens as well as peasants. It took many years to become the quintessential English drink!

Tea Past

Can you imagine a breakfast consisting of cold meats, fish, cheeses, and ale or beer at six thirty in the morning? That's what the early seventeenth-century wealthy people of England ate and drank at the time. For those less than wealthy, a piece of bread with syrup or, worse yet, a bowlful of pottage and a pint of ale to wash it down were commonplace. Tea wasn't considered the beverage of choice until much later in the century, and even then, only the wealthy were able to partake of it because of its steep price tag.

Tea arrived in London in 1657, but the cost of tea kept it from being widely known until much later. Not until the Portuguese Catherine of Braganza arrived in England to marry Charles II did tea drinking come into vogue. The marriage, arranged partially to help pay off the debt that Charles II had inherited, came with a large dowry, some of which was tea. Tea was a favorite drink of the Portuguese court, and Catherine brought it with her to England. It has been said that the first thing the soon-to-be queen asked for as she got off the ship in May of 1662 was a cup of tea. Tea drinking soon became fashionable and spread from the ladies of the court to the aristocratic social circles and then to the wealthy classes.

Established coffee shops were among the first merchants to sell tea in England. At that time, coffee shops were places only men were allowed to enter. They were full of smoke, noise, and unpleasant smells—and off-limits to the ladies. In 1717, the Twining family opened The Golden Lyon, a tea shop next door to their existing coffee shop. This new shop, which sold teas, allowed ladies to enter and make their own purchases.

Tea caught on among all the classes, but the taxes on tea were so high in that day that it was unaffordable to most. This led to smuggling. Smugglers brought the tea into the country, avoided payment of the duty tax, and sold it much cheaper. At one time in the late eighteenth century, many believed that more tea was imported through illegal methods than through legal channels. To make matters worse, smugglers began compromising the purity of the tea by mixing it with leaves from other plants; thus, stretching their supply and increasing their profits.

Green tea was easier to adulterate than black tea. Often additives, which included poisonous chemicals, were mixed in with the tainted green teas. For example, after diluting the green tea with other plant leaves, smugglers used a metallic paint to make sure the tea was the correct shade of green. The public soon caught on to this trickery, and black tea became more popular than green. Some of those who complained about the effects tea was having on their nerves were probably being poisoned! The government intervened in 1785 and lowered the duty tax considerably to make tea more affordable. This measure soon wiped out the illegal smuggling activity.

In most homes, tea slowly replaced ale or beer at breakfast time, and I can only guess that it was a welcome change! As was common during this era, the lady of the house would brew the tea. For those that could afford it, white sugar and milk were added for flavor. Tea was also enjoyed after dinner in the drawing room. Although the women were the ones that most often gathered to drink the tea, sometimes the men would join them later. Serving tea to visiting guests also was becoming more popular.

During certain seasons of the year, London's public gardens became quite the hot spots of activity. The gardens were places not only for enjoying beautiful scenery and invigorating walks but also for such activities as horseback riding, circus performances, boat rides, and drinking tea. Places to play games and dance could also be found in the gardens.

The nineteenth century brought a new kind of tea to England. Up until then, all tea was imported from China through the English East India Company. Because trade had become strained and several uprisings had occurred between China and England, England began to look for other sources to supply their beloved and now needed tea. The tea plant was discovered growing wild in the British territory of India and, after much work, Indian tea was brought to England in 1839. Ceylon, another British territory now known as Sri Lanka, also started growing tea. At that time, the tea exported from both of those countries was exclusively black. Because India and Ceylon were British territories, the cost to import tea from these regions was much lower, and tea prices came down. Thus, England became a predominantly black tea drinking nation.

Mealtimes of the 1800's had changed a bit from previous centuries. On a typical day, breakfast was served between 8:00 and 9:00 in the morning, and the main meal of the day was served at 7:30 or later in the evening. This left a large gap in the day without a meal, so a newly created light meal became commonplace. It was known as *luncheon*, *nuncheon*, or as Jane Austen liked to call it in her writings, *noonshine*. With lunch being a light meal and dinner still six or more hours away, what we now know as afternoon teatime came into practice.

Anna, seventh Duchess of Bedford, is credited with "inventing" afternoon tea, but it is believed that many others were partaking of tea in the afternoon at this time in history. As the story goes, in 1841 Anna had asked that tea and something to eat (probably some bread and butter) be brought to her bedroom because she was experiencing a sinking feeling (most likely hunger pains). She soon began to invite friends to share in her afternoon repast of tea and snacks.

Afternoon tea was also referred to as "Low Tea" because the guests were comfortably seated in low chairs with arms, and the tea was served on side tables or coffee tables. The idea spread through the upper and middle class as a way for women to entertain their friends and gossip. The meal grew a bit grander and often included crustless finger sandwiches, scones, and desserts. Those without great means in the middle class still managed to have afternoon tea, but they would do it "potluck" style to conserve funds.

The working class also enjoyed their tea but did so in a different fashion. England's industrial revolution required the working class to spend long hours in factories or mines, and that left no time for frivolous entertainment. They developed their own teatime—known as "High Tea." The name reflected the height of the kitchen or dining room table where the tea was served. Occurring at the end of a long workday with hungry appetites in mind, this meal was also known as a "Meat Tea." It always included strong tea and, depending upon each household, a variety of cheeses, potted pies, cold meats, bacon, bread, and desserts. It was just what the hardworking people needed as they gathered with their family after a strenuous day's labor. High tea was adopted by others beyond the working class after a time. Those of the upper class who employed servants allowed them to have Sundays off. Putting together a

high tea without the help of their servants was easy for the wealthy crowd—they simply placed their leftovers on the sideboard. The types of food served, however, were a bit more luxurious and plentiful than those offered by the working class.

As the popularity of tea grew, an enterprising London business saw a need and acted on it. In 1884, the Aerated Bread Company thought up the idea to turn one of their unused rooms into a tearoom. The idea was so popular that the company opened many more such tearooms in the surrounding area. Soon thereafter numerous other companies followed suit and opened their own tearooms. These shops, unlike the coffee shops of the day, were clean and allowed women to sit inside comfortably and enjoy sipping tea. Tearooms also gave women a proper place to gather outside the home without a male escort and keep her reputation intact.

Soon after the tea shops opened and going out to tea became fashionable, high-end hotels opened tea lounges or palm courts to serve tea to visitors in the afternoon. By the early 1900s, as the Argentinean tango craze swept the country, tea dances at hotels and clubs became very popular. The craze slowed down after the 1920s, but some establishments, such as the Waldorf, tried to keep the tradition alive until World War II began.

With the inception of the war, the need to ration food and supplies, including tea, became necessary. Because tea was not abundant, it was treasured all the more. Some, civilian and military alike, even considered it to be

the country's secret weapon—a few believed it to be more important than ammunition.

The rationing of tea continued after the war and until 1952. Then the American-style fast-food establishments began to creep into England. Although the British still drank tea at home, tearooms and the practice of going out for tea came to an end. The era of convenience had taken over, and fast-food restaurants replaced the tearooms. Soon thereafter, the tea bag was introduced, and it changed the way the English brewed their tea.

TEA PRESENT

Maybe the English got tired of everything "to go" and the fast-paced lifestyle that had overtaken their culture. For whatever reason, in the early 1980s, a tea renaissance began. The practice of taking afternoon tea spread, and visitors from other countries soon arrived in England, where it all began. This prompted new businesses to open and hotels to rethink the way they served tea. An interest in tea dances came back, and hotels such as

the Waldorf and the Ritz started holding weekend tea dances again.

England is still considered to be a tea drinking nation—on average, 165 million cups are consumed daily. Although many drink coffee, the most popular beverage is tea. According to the United Kingdom Tea Council, Britain is the second largest nation of tea drinkers per capita (Ireland is first). Although 96 percent of the tea brewed in England is brewed using a tea bag, which was introduced in the 1960s, the practice is changing a bit. Just as in the United States, fine loose-leaf teas are being introduced.

In response to the need to increase the quality of tea establishments across Britain, the United Kingdom Tea Council established The Tea Guild in 1985. The Tea Guild's main goal is to help recognize and promote those tea businesses that have achieved high standards. The invitation-only membership keeps these high standards in place by sending "secret shoppers" to call upon interested businesses. If the secret shoppers decide that the tea business is worthy of membership, they are invited to join.

The Tea Guild also goes undercover and samples the tea in tearooms and hotels across the country. Each year these anonymous judges then vote on Britain's top tea places based on such criteria as service, décor, cleanliness, ambience, and the choice and quality of the tea. It is quite an honor to make this prestigious list. The guild then publishes the list in a guidebook for those interested in finding the best places to have tea in all of England.

MAKING TEA ENGLISH STYLE

Making tea is not a fussy thing in England. According to my friend Jane Pettigrew*, a tea specialist who lives in London, most people use tea bags, placing them either in a teapot or directly into a mug. The adventurist uses loose-leaf tea.

Black tea is the most widespread type of tea brewed—this has been the tradition for quite some time. The most familiar types of tea are an English breakfast, Earl Grey, or some other type of strong black tea. Jane, along with other tea enthusiasts in her country, is trying to change the way the English brew their tea. If you want to replicate the English way of brewing tea but add some pizzazz and extra flavor, place quality loose-leaf black tea in a paper filter* or infuser basket*, set the filter or infuser basket in a mug or teapot, add boiling water, and allow the leaves to steep for three to five minutes, depending on how strong you like it. Be sure to remove the leaves after steeping for optimal flavor.

It is very English to add milk and sugar to the tea—both go nicely with the commonly used Indian and Ceylon teas. The amount of milk and sugar is a personal preference. However, whether the milk goes in before the tea or after the tea is an etiquette controversy, and I believe this debate will continue. According to the training I received while attaining my Tea and Etiquette® certification* under the direction of Dorothea Johnson, this issue needs to be put to rest. Ms. Johnson believes strongly that the tea is poured first, and the milk follows. She has many reasons for stating this, but the one that I found most memorable was that the Queen of England does it this way. If the Queen pours her tea first and then adds the milk, it must be proper—wouldn't you agree? So if you are ever invited to have tea with the Queen, avoid an etiquette faux pas and prepare your tea her way! A thin lemon slice could be added for flavor but never in conjunction with the milk. Adding lemon is not as common as adding milk and sugar.

TEATIME IN ENGLAND

In England tea is served with all meals and as a snack. It is also served at work breaks and into the evening. It is a part of the British culture, and most homes have tea in their pantries. In some regions of the country, particularly among certain groups in the north, the evening meal is referred to as *tea* instead of *supper* or *dinner* even though tea is usually not served at all!

I love to entertain with tea in a variety of ways. I chose to feature recipes for a high tea for several reasons. I thought it would help dispel the confusion between high tea and afternoon tea. Also I love to have tea with my husband, and although he has afternoon tea with me on occasion, he usually needs to eat before we go because his appetite is not as easily satisfied as mine. Lastly, my ancestors from England were probably among the working class, and I can tell you that hasn't changed with my generation. My family is not royalty. Nor are we aristocrats in any sense other than at tea parties and dress-up time when my daughter was younger. I thought it would be fun to have a tea that is male friendly and full of hearty foods—one that everyone could enjoy and leave satisfied and contented. Feel free to add a platter of English cheeses such as cheddar, blue Stilton, and Cheshire to the meal. Include artisan crackers or freshly baked bread from home or a bakery to serve with the cheese.

The first three recipes were inspired by my friend Kim Jordy*, owner of the wonderful tearoom Tea Leaves and Thyme in Woodstock, Georgia. Kim's mother, Jillian Taylor, was from London and has many fond memories of preparing and serving the following recipes.

RECIPES

Shepherd's Pie or Cottage pie

Shepherd's pie is usually made with ground lamb or roast and cottage pie is usually made with ground beef or roast. Kim Jordy's mom made her pies with leftover roast beef because her children did not care for lamb. As a child, Kim remembers how fun it was to put the roast through the meat grinder. Now Kim uses that same grinder to make her own shepherd's and cottage pies.

1½ pounds ground beef (or lamb) roast or 1½ pounds cooked ground beef (or lamb)
2 pounds (3 large) russet potatoes, peeled and cubed
¼ to ½ cup milk
2 tablespoons butter
1 bag frozen peas and carrots thawed
1 tablespoon cooking oil
1 onion, chopped fine
salt and pepper to taste

Preheat oven to 350 degrees. Boil potatoes in salted water for 15 minutes. Meanwhile, sauté onion in cooking oil until soft. Drain potatoes and place them into a large bowl. Add ¼ cup milk and the butter to the potatoes and mash them until almost smooth. Add additional milk if too dry. Place the cooked meat in the bottom of a 9 x 9 or a 9 x13 pan and layer the cooked, chopped onion over the meat. Sprinkle the thawed carrots and peas over the meat mixture. Top with the mashed potatoes and bake for 30 minutes. Garnish with paprika if desired. Serves 6.

Meringue Kisses

As a child, Kim looked forward to eating this special treat at Christmastime. She has continued the Christmas tradition and now bakes them for her children!

2 egg whites, room temperature
½ teaspoon salt
⅛ teaspoon cream of tartar
1 teaspoon vanilla
½ to ¾ cup sugar, depending how sweet you like your meringues

Preheat oven to 400 degrees. Beat egg whites in a stainless steel bowl. Add salt and cream of tarter and continue to beat mixture until it forms stiff peaks. Add sugar 1 tablespoon at a time, beating well after each addition. Then add vanilla and mix until combined. Line a cookie sheet with parchment paper. Place meringue mixture into a piping bag with a star tip and press through to make one-inch stars. Set the cookie sheet into the oven and *turn off the oven*. After 30 minutes, use a wooden spoon to prop the oven door open and leave the cookie sheet in the oven overnight. Remove the kisses from the cookie sheet the next day and store in an airtight container. To bake meringue kisses in one day, place them in a preheated oven set at 225 degrees and bake for 1½ hours. Then, turn off the oven and allow the kisses to cool in the closed oven for another ½ hour or until dry. Note: These are best made when it is not humid outside.

Crumb Ginger Cake

This recipe was my (Lisa Boalt Richardson's) great-grandmother Effie Johnson Smelser's recipe and has been passed down through and baked by four generations. Effie was known for her cooking abilities, which enabled her to be a live-in cook for many prominent people in her town prior to marrying in 1911.

2 cups all-purpose flour
1 cup granulated sugar
½ to 1 teaspoon powdered ginger (amount depends on personal taste— I use a full teaspoon)
1 teaspoon cinnamon
½ cup salted butter, chilled and cut into small pieces
1 teaspoon baking soda
½ teaspoon salt
1 egg
2 tablespoons dark molasses
1 teaspoon vanilla
1 cup buttermilk
fresh whipped cream to serve with cake

Preheat oven to 350 degrees. Combine flour, sugar, ginger, and cinnamon. Cut in butter using a pastry cutter until mixture resembles the consistency of cornmeal. You may also use a food processor and pulse slowly until mixture is the desired consistency. Take out 1 cup of mixture and set aside for topping. Add soda, salt, egg, molasses, vanilla, and buttermilk to the remaining mixture. Mix well with an electric mixer or by hand. Grease

an 8-inch square baking dish with cooking spray and pour the batter into it. Sprinkle the reserved crumb mixture over the batter and bake for 20 to 25 minutes or until the cake is set. Serve warm with fresh whipped cream.

Sausage and Mash (also known as Bangers and Mash)

Whenever Kim's grandmother and Aunt Sheilia came for a visit, they brought English tinned sausage. Kim could barely wait for them to unpack their bags so they could prepare this recipe for dinner.

2 pounds potatoes, peeled and cubed
2 teaspoons salt
4 tablespoons butter
¼ to ½ cup milk
2 pounds banger sausage* or raw pork sausage links
cooking oil
flour
parsley

Place the potatoes in a large pot and fill with cold water. Add salt to the water, cover the pot, and cook the potatoes until soft, about 20 minutes. Remove from heat, drain well, and pour into a large bowl. Add butter and milk to the potatoes and whip with an electric mixer until stiff peaks form. Keep warm. Place a large frying pan over medium heat and add enough cooking oil to cover the bottom of the pan. Dip sausages into flour and set them into the hot oil. Fry the sausages gently, turning often, until evenly cooked throughout and the flour crust is golden brown—at least 20 minutes. To serve, pile the mashed potatoes in the center of a large platter and stack the sausages neatly on top of the potatoes. To garnish, place parsley along the side of the potatoes or chop it up and sprinkle on top. Serves 6.

Kenya

"I had a farm in Africa," is one of the beginning lines spoken by Meryl Streep in the movie *Out of Africa*. She plays a character based on the real-life story of Karen Blixen and her plight in the British protectorate of Kenya in 1913. Baroness Blixen experienced difficulties with her coffee farm partly because it was located at a high altitude. Perhaps she might have been more successful growing tea because tea grows well at high altitudes!

Toward the end of the movie, which was filmed just outside of Nairobi, Kenya, the Baroness invites Lord Delamere to her home after her coffee beans have all been destroyed in a fire. She tells him, "We are just out of coffee, but I can give you some tea." It is a great movie to set the mood and understand what the times and conditions were like when the first tea farms began in Kenya.

TEA PAST

Kenya is a country situated in East Africa along the Equator. It borders Tanzania, Uganda, Sudan, Somalia, and the India Ocean. It has many landmarks such as the snow-capped Mt. Kenya and the Savanna, which is the home to fabulous wildlife, great for safari adventures, and bordered by a beautiful coastline with sandy beaches. The Great Rift Valley, another Kenyan landmark, runs through the country and divides the tea growing regions.

Kenya has struggled for its independence for centuries. In the late 1800s, the British wanted control of the country because of the trade alliances and the fertile highland region. A railway was built from the coastal city of Mombasa inland toward Lake Victoria. When the railway was completed in 1906, thousands of white European settlers flocked to the country to establish coffee, tobacco, and tea plantations. The natives were forced to move off their land. The territory became a British Crown Colony in 1920, and the name was changed to Kenya Colony.

Tea was introduced in Kenya by a European man named G.W.L. Caine in 1903. Caine brought tea plants for ornamental purposes, and some are still alive and growing strong today.

In 1904, Mr. Arnold Butler McDonell, better known as A.B., came to Kenya from England to work at a forest station. He acquired a team of oxen and dragged logs from the forest to a sawmill. The sawed logs called *sleepers* were used to build the railway. He married in 1908 and soon after started a family.

The British government tried to get settlers to move to Kenya by selling the land very cheaply. A.B. took the government up on their offer and bought 350 acres. He built a house, started a farm just outside of Nairobi, and named it *Kiambethu**, which means "traditional dancing ground."

A.B. tried several different kinds of crops, such as corn, flax, and coffee, all to no avail. At 7200 feet, the altitude of the farm was too high to grow coffee—probably the same plight Baroness Blixen had with her farm.

He tried tea in 1918 after a friend sent him some tea seeds from India. He planted 20 acres and by 1926, he was selling his tea. All of the processing was done on site. He hired the Kikuyu (native people of the land) to pluck the leaves. The Kikuyu women would then pound the withered tea in hollowed-out tree trunks, similar to a giant mortar and pestle system with a pole. The tea leaves were left to dry in the sun or by charcoal heaters if it wasn't sunny.

A.B.'s four daughters sold most of Kiambethu Farm in 1992 because it got to be too much work for them in their elder years. However, they kept the 30 acres that

surrounded their house and the forested area where the indigenous colobus monkeys had made their homes.

TEA PRESENT

Kenya's growing region has expanded over the years. The Great Rift Valley runs north and south and is just west of Nairobi. Tea grows in the Eastern Rift Valley and the Western Rift Valley and has become one of the country's main exports. Kenya is vying to be the world's number one exporter of tea. The tea is sent primarily to the Middle East and the United Kingdom. Although the majority of the tea produced is black, Kenya has begun processing green and other types of tea in the last few years.

Kenya has only become a tea drinking nation since the English occupation occurred. Their tea drinking style is of course British, but it has a distinctive African flair. Advertising campaigns promote tea, and to most Kenyans "anytime is teatime."

In the workplace, tea is the beverage of choice for breaks—not coffee as it is here in the United States. In Kenya, if the company you work for has more than just a handful of people, a woman is hired to make tea for the employees. She comes around with a trolley and serves tea all day to the workers and management.

Tours can be taken of the Kiambethu Farm. They are directed by Fiona and Marcus Vernon, who are the third generation to live in the home on the farm. When you pull up to the very English looking cottage, you may see a monkey or two sitting atop the home, a vivid reminder that you are still in Africa and not England. The tour is a half-day adventure, which naturally starts with a cup of tea. The process of making tea is explained, and then there is an opportunity to see some of the tea fields. Following that, the tour includes a beautiful walk through the indigenous forest with a Kenyan guide who explains the wild flora and fauna. The adventure continues back at the house. A pre-lunch drink is served while you linger on the veranda and take in the views of the Ngong Hills. On a clear day, you may see Kilimanjaro. Lunch includes vegetables from their garden and desserts topped with fresh cream from their herd of Channel Island cows.

MAKING TEA KENYAN STYLE

In Kenya tea is made in different ways depending on the region and what tribe or social class you are from. One way to steep tea is in a saucepan. Add three teaspoons of black Kenyan tea to two cups of water and heat until it boils. Then add two cups of milk and four to six teaspoons of sugar, depending upon how sweet you like your tea. Let the mixture come to a boil again and then remove it from the heat. Strain out the tea leaves and pour the liquid into a kettle or teapot. Some like to add the milk to the tea leaves and water and let it all come to a boil.

Another way to make tea is in a teapot. Depending on the size of your teapot, use one teaspoon black tea for each cup of water. Place tea leaves in the teapot and add boiling water. Steep the tea for three to five minutes. After the preferred steeping time is finished, use a strainer and pour the brew into teacups. Cover a second teapot full of boiling water with a tea cozy. Use this teapot to steep the leaves again or weaken the brew a bit for those who don't like their tea so strong.

Depending on personal preferences, milk, sugar, or lemon can be used to add flavor to the tea.

When preparing tea Kenyan style, be prepared to make plenty. It is considered rude to run out of tea while entertaining guests. Depending upon the region and social status, guests might be served tea in large mugs. It is the hostess' responsibility to keep the mugs topped off as long as the guests remain. The guest of honor is given the largest mug to ensure proper respect. In other regions or social classes, tea is served English style using a china teapot, delicate teacups, and saucers.

Whichever way you decide to serve your tea, serve it with plenty of hospitality. Tea is not only grown in Kenya, but it is the local tradition to serve and consume it with generous portions of hospitality. So brew plenty and enjoy!

CULTURAL TIP:

When preparing tea Kenyan style, be prepared to make plenty. It is considered rude to run out of tea while entertaining guests. It is the hostess' responsibility to keep the mugs topped off as long as the guests remain. The guest of honor is given the largest mug to ensure proper respect.

TEATIME IN KENYA

A visit to anyone's home in Kenya begins with an offer of a cup of tea. Here tea is referred to as *chai*. Except for the coastal regions where Indian influences might be felt and masala spices might be added, *chai* is not typically served with the spices associated with chai tea served in the United States. The traditional tea served is black.

Tea is enjoyed throughout the day. It is always served hot no matter how warm the weather. It is served with breakfast and after lunch and dinner. Even if other drinks are offered with a meal, tea will always be offered last. Morning tea breaks happen around 10:00, and an afternoon tea break occurs every afternoon about 4:00. Sipping a nightcap of tea before bed is not uncommon! It is said that a meal is not complete unless you have had tea to finish and wash everything down.

Teatime is observed from 4:00 to 6:00 each afternoon in all the best hotels, country clubs, and sports clubs across the nation. Kenya tea is typically strong, and so it makes sense that tea is served with milk and sugar. Their way of tea was probably adopted from their British roots.

Throughout the last few years, David Walker, of Walker Tea, has become a friend and colleague of mine. He came and spoke at a Southern Association of Tea Businesses* meeting a few years back. He has provided a wealth of information to me about not only Kenya teas, but tea in general. As a child Walker went to school with some of the grandchildren of the owners of Kiambethu Farm. He began his work in 1965 as an apprentice immediately after finishing agriculture college and has continued in all aspects of tea from the grower to the cup. He now works as a tea consultant In Europe and countries such as Bolivia, Kenya, and America.

Walker shared these recipes with me so that we all can enjoy an afternoon tea Kenya style. Along with the delicious scone, bread, and dessert recipes, you could add such fruits as pineapples, papayas, citruses of any kind, and miniature bananas. You can serve these separately or make a fruit salad. The fruit will complement the menu well.

RECIPES

Savory Honey Scones

2 1/4 teaspoons rosemary, finely chopped and divided
1 1/3 cups all-purpose flour
1 1/3 cups semolina
2 teaspoons baking powder
1/2 teaspoon baking soda
1/2 teaspoon coarse salt
6 ounces soft goat cheese, chilled and crumbled into bits
1/4 cup honey
1/2 cup heavy cream, divided
1 egg

Preheat oven to 425 degrees. In a large bowl, mix 2 teaspoons rosemary with all other dry ingredients. Add goat cheese to the dry ingredients and set aside. Whisk together honey, half the cream, and egg. Stir this mixture into the dry ingredients until a soft dough forms. Form dough into a ball. Turn out onto a floured surface and separate the dough into 2 equal portions and pat each portion into a circle about 3/4-inch thick. Cut into 8 wedges. Separate and arrange wedges on a baking sheet. Brush tops with remaining cream and sprinkle with remaining rosemary. Place in oven and bake 10 to 12 minutes or until golden brown. It is yummy to serve these with butter, honey, and/or softened goat cheese!

Marmalade Bread

3 cups all-purpose flour, sifted
1 tablespoon baking powder
⅓ cup sugar
1 teaspoon salt
¼ teaspoon baking soda
1 1-pound jar orange marmalade
1 egg, beaten
1 teaspoon vanilla
¾ cup orange juice
1 tablespoon orange zest
¼ cup light olive oil
1 cup walnuts

Preheat oven to 350 degrees. Sift together dry ingredients in a large bowl and set aside. After reserving ¼ cup marmalade, in a separate bowl combine remaining marmalade, egg, juice, vanilla, zest, and oil. Add this to the flour mixture, stirring just until moist. Stir in nuts. Spread batter into a greased 9½ x 5 x 3-inch loaf pan. Bake for 1 hour. Remove from pan and place on baking sheet. Spread top of loaf with remaining marmalade and place it back in the oven for 1 to 2 minutes. Remove loaf from oven and allow to cool. Note: You may use smaller loaf pans to bake this bread, but if you do, reduce your baking time to 40 to 45 minutes or until set.

Cherry Puffs

9 ounces pitted frozen cherries, thawed and drained
3 tablespoons black cherry jam or preserves
¼ teaspoon almond extract
2 10-ounce packages butter puff pastry shells
    (may also use mini shells for smaller serving size)
2 tablespoons almonds, ground
powdered sugar for tops of puffs (optional)

Preheat oven to 400 degrees. Bake shells according to package directions and allow to cool. Meanwhile, combine cherries and cherry conserve together in a saucepan until warm and mixed well. Take off heat and add almond extract. Spoon a few ground almonds into each cooled shell and then spoon cherry mixture on top of the almonds. Sift powdered sugar on top if you like. You may serve these warm or at room temperature.

Russia

The Russian tea philosophy is "teatime is all the time." Although tea is deeply embedded in Russian culture, that has not always been the case. Prior to tea, *sbiten*, a brew of hot water, honey, and herbs, was the drink of choice.

TEA PAST

It wasn't until the beginning of the seventeenth century that Russia began to import tea from China. Caravans of hundreds of camels made the long journey across roughly 11,000 miles of barren and mountainous terrain. It took over a year for the tea to reach Russia, and the tea supply was limited to what could be carried on camelback. Given these conditions, the price of tea was so high that only the wealthy could afford such a luxury.

In 1735, Czarina Elizabeth established a regular private caravan trade, and the price of tea fell. It is said that by 1796, Russia was drinking more than 3.5 million pounds of tea a year. Finally around 1900, the Trans-Siberian Railroad was opened, and that put the camel caravans out of business. The train carried much more tea at one time than the camels could, and the trip was shortened to about two months. Because more tea was available more quickly, the price fell again. Now everyone was able to afford the once-thought-of-as-a-luxury drink. Tea has been a mainstay for Russian life ever since.

With all this tea drinking, the samovar was introduced.

The samovar is believed to be adopted from the Mongolian firepot. Synonymous with Russian tea drinking, the samovar combines a hot water heater and a teapot. The older versions were coal fired, but the new ones run on electricity. The lower unit is a cross between an urn and a kettle.

Water is boiled and then poured out via a spigot. The teapot rests on the top and stays warm by using heat from the lower portion. Tea is made into a very strong concentration called a *zavarka* and then diluted with water from the lower portion. This ingenious contraption allowed Russians to keep a hot pot of tea going all day long.

Russians traditionally use special glass teacups with silver holders to sip their tea. The holders are decorated with engraved pictures and enamel elements. This Russian tradition can be observed when traveling by train through the Russian countryside.

TEA PRESENT

Russia is the largest country in Europe and is about twice the size of the United States. It shares a border with China and Mongolia. Because it is located so far to the north, Russian winters are long and cold.

Tea is hearty and warm and fits right into the Russian lifestyle. The tea culture of modern Russia has changed slightly, but consumption has not decreased. Tea is considered the national beverage alongside vodka and is served from morning till night.

Tea is always served hot in Russia. One would not think to add ice to tea! As soon as a child is old enough to sit at the table, the child is old enough to drink tea with the family. It is said by Russians that "tea completes

CULTURAL TIP:

When a guest stops by for a visit, it would be considered rude not to offer the guest a place to sit and have tea. The term "having tea" never means just drinking the infusion. "Having tea" to a Russian means having tea with some food—a small snack or a dessert or a full meal. Whatever you can conjure up from your kitchen and how much time you and your guest have defines "having tea."

the deal," meaning tea is used to finish a meal. Tea also puts a different accent on a snack. It turns a snack into a mini meal and allows you to sit down and relax for a bit.

When a guest stops by for a visit, it would be considered rude not to offer the guest a place to sit and have tea. This has been passed down from generation to generation and is well-embedded in the culture. The term "having tea" never means just drinking the infusion. "Having tea" to a Russian means having tea with some food—a small snack or a dessert or a full meal. Whatever you can conjure up from your kitchen and how much time you and your guest have defines "having tea."

MAKING TEA RUSSIAN STYLE

Even if a Russian family does not own a samovar, they still make their tea with the traditional and highly concentrated brew. But instead of serving it from the samovar, they serve it from a porcelain teapot. Black tea is the tea of choice. Instead of placing one teaspoon of tea leaves per cup of water in a teapot, measure one teaspoon of leaves per guest and place the leaves into the teapot. Pour boiling water into the teapot and steep about five minutes. Because the tea leaves are typically left in the teapot, use a strainer to pour a small amount of this tea concentrate into each person's cup. Fill a second teapot with boiling water. Use this water to dilute each cup of

brew depending on the person's personal taste.

Commonly sugar, lemon, and sometimes honey are added to this tea. Some still enjoy putting sugar cubes in their mouths and sipping their tea. It is interesting that Russian tea is usually not a flavored tea, so every now and then some enjoy spooning in freshly mashed raspberries or black currants. On occasion *varenye*, a dark cherry preserve, is served in little bowls with the tea. A person first spoons the *varenye* into their mouth and follows it up with a sip of tea. I guess this would be considered their version of a private fruit blend.

Don't be concerned if you don't own a samovar or the delicate glass cups with silver holders. A couple porcelain teapots and teacups will do the trick. If you want to treat yourself to something special, consider purchasing the blue and white tea set* featured in this chapter. It is made by the Russian Lomonosov (Imperial) Porcelain factory, which is one of the oldest porcelain manufacturers in Europe. It dates back to 1744 and was founded by Peter the Great's daughter, Empress Elizabeth. The beautiful pattern is Cobalt Net. It is made entirely by hand and is decorated with 22 karat gold!

You might want to play some Russian music in the background to feel the Russian spirit. A Russian tea party is not about being stuffy or uptight. It's about enjoying the company of others and being full of cheer.

TEATIME IN RUSSIA

Russian dishes are made primarily with carbohydrates and fat and very little protein. Food is grown in the region and consists of grains and root vegetables such as potatoes and onions. Fresh bread is a staple of their diet, and if you live in the city, you buy it every day from a local baker. If you live in the country, you make it fresh daily.

Because Russia's teatime is all the time, there isn't one specific meal or food related to having tea. A typical day begins with a breakfast served with tea first thing in the morning. Dinner is served about 3:00 in the afternoon and is considered the largest meal of the day. Tea follows dinner. Supper is served around 8:00 in the evening. It is usually a lighter meal and followed by tea and sometimes dessert. The Russians commonly sip on tea throughout the day and sometimes add a small snack.

To recreate Russian teatime is not that difficult. For a simple version, serve a light snack with tea Russian style—use the concentrated brew from one teapot and the boiling water from another. Consider offering an open-faced sandwich using crusty French bread. Serve it with honey, butter, and strawberry preserves. To make the snack a little more substantial, prepare the sandwiches with sliced salami and cheese.

To recreate a suppertime tea, prepare the tea the same way but serve it after the meal with dessert. A wonderful menu for an evening tea might include *pierogies*. These can either be made to be savory or sweet and may be used as the main course or dessert. Serving a noodle *babka* filled with sugar and raisins for dessert is also a good idea for an evening tea.

All of these recipes have been given to me by my friend Yelena, who is from Russia.

Easy Russian Cheese Sandwiches

crusty French bread, sliced
unsalted butter
Havarti or Cheddar cheese, sliced

Lightly spread butter on sliced bread. Place cheese between two slices and serve.

Easy Russian Salami Sandwiches

Fresh-baked artisan bread, sliced
unsalted butter
salami, sliced

Lightly spread butter on sliced bread. Place salami between two slices and serve.

*R*ECIPES

Pierogies

Pierogies can be made savory or sweet. Instead of making homemade dough, Yelena takes a shortcut and uses canned crescent rolls, canned pizza dough, or canned biscuits.

Mushroom and Potato Filling

2 medium potatoes, peeled and cut into quarters
¼ cup heavy cream
1 teaspoon salt, divided
3 tablespoons unsalted butter, divided
1 tablespoon cooking oil
1 8-ounce package white mushrooms, cleaned and sliced thinly
½ cup sweet onion, chopped

Boil potatoes in salted water for about 10 minutes or until soft. Drain the potatoes. Using a potato masher, mash potatoes until smooth. Add cream, ½ teaspoon salt, and 2 tablespoons butter. Stir until mixed well and creamy. Set aside. Meanwhile, place 1 tablespoon cooking oil and 1 tablespoon butter into a sauté pan and heat. When butter has melted, add chopped onion, sliced mushrooms, and ½ teaspoon salt and cook over medium heat until soft and all the liquid has been cooked out. Add the onion and mushroom mixture to the mashed potatoes and stir well.

Cheese Filling

Farmer's cheese, thinly sliced
raisins (optional)

Slice cheese into small slices. and add to dough. Sprinkle with raisins if you choose.

Fruit Filling

strawberries, washed, dried well, and thinly sliced
  or blueberries, washed, dried well
sugar

Add a heaping tablespoon of fruit to dough and sprinkle with a small amount of sugar.

To assemble pierogies, begin by preheating the oven to 350 degrees. Place dough onto a large cutting board that has been lightly dusted with flour. Roll dough out until approximately ⅛ inch thick. Using a 4-inch diameter glass or cookie cutter, cut the dough into circles.

> Note: If using canned biscuit dough, divide each biscuit in half and then roll each of the two sections into 4-inch circles. If using canned crescent roll dough, pinch the seams together before rolling out and cutting into circles.

Place a heaping teaspoon of potato and mushroom filling or a slice of cheese (and optional raisins) or a heaping tablespoon of sugar-dusted fruit onto the center of a circle of dough. Fold the circle in half and seal the edges by hand or by using the back of a fork. Place pierogies on a greased cookie sheet, brush tops with beaten egg wash, and bake 18 to 22 minutes or until tops are golden brown.

Noodle Babka

1 16-ounce package angel hair pasta
7 eggs, beaten well
¾ cup sugar
1 teaspoon vanilla
4 tablespoons butter, melted
½ cup heavy cream
1 cup raisins, soaked in boiling water for 5 minutes and then
  drained well

Preheat oven to 350 degrees. Cook pasta according to directions and then drain and rinse well in cold water to remove all the starch. Put pasta back into the pot, add melted butter, toss together, and set aside. In a large bowl, mix beaten eggs, cream, sugar, vanilla, and soaked and drained raisins. Add in buttered pasta and stir until well combined. Pour mixture into a greased 9 x 13 pan and bake 45 minutes or until golden brown. Serve warm with a garnish of apricot or strawberry preserves.

Iran

Iran is known for its beautiful Persian rugs, but there is much more to this country than their carpets. Persia, as it was called before 1935, has a culture rich in philosophy, art, science, and religion. Its history dates back three thousand years, and at one time, it was an empire that stretched from India all the way to the Mediterranean. Influenced by immigrants who have come to call it home, this area is a melting pot of many cultures. Some of these cultures include the ancient Babylonians, Assyrians, Greeks, Romans, and Turks.

Likewise, Persian food, the food of Iran, has wonderful influences from all of these regions as well as from India and Russia. Tea is the national beverage—evident in the number of teahouses spread from one end of the country to the other. However, that has not always been the case. Coffee was the brew of choice at one time. This is apparent in the fact that some teahouses are still called coffeehouses, but serve mainly tea. Tea is known as *cha'i* in Farsi, the language of Iran.

TEA PAST

The history of tea in Iran dates back to the end of the fifteenth century when Mongols most likely brought it into the country through a large trade route known as the Silk Route or Silk Road. This route stretches across five thousand land and sea miles and connects east, south, and western Asia with the Mediterranean world, including Africa and Europe. Not only was silk traded, but tea, spices, and jewels, as well as knowledge, ideas, and cultures were all exchanged along that route. Because tea was easier to obtain than coffee through the trade routes and because the Mongol influence was growing, tea began replacing coffee in popularity.

As demand for tea grew, more and more people became interested in farming tea. Failed attempts at growing tea from seeds from India are noted as early as the mid 1800s. By 1899, tea farming using saplings from India was introduced again. The small plants were planted in the northern regions of Iran, south of the Caspian Sea. The tea did well in this region's climate, and farms soon expanded in this area. The people of Iran have, for the most part, been the consumers of their own tea, and very little of it, if any, has ever been exported. In fact, despite growing their own tea, Iran must import more tea from other countries to meet demands.

Tea could be considered a national pastime in the country and has become deeply embedded into the culture. The Persian style of drinking tea shows the influence of and the connection with Russia. The samovar, most likely brought to Iran by Russian traders, was and still is a very common kitchen "appliance" in Persian households. Making tea with the samovar continues to this day.

TEA PRESENT

Consumption of tea has grown over the years and plays a social role in Iran. It is served everywhere and consumed throughout the day. It would be unheard of not to offer your guests a cup of tea upon their arrival to your home.

As I began to study the traditions and tea drinking practices of Iran, I came across an interesting cultural etiquette custom known as *tarof*. As a student and teacher of etiquette, I always find other cultures' etiquette intriguing. My Iranian friends have confirmed this practice, and although most think it is silly, those who are considered to have good manners must still practice it. *Tarof* is a way of showing modesty, dignity, and restraint in a back and forth gesture between two parties. *Tarof* is demonstrated by always refusing to eat something when first asked.

When offered tea in Iran, you are most likely going to be offered a treat of some kind called *shirini*. To show good manners, you should refuse the treat politely even if you desire it and are hungry. The host must then be more insistent in offering you the treat, and you must more emphatically but politely turn it down. By the third time, the host will practically put the treats on a plate and hand it to you. You may then accept the offer and enjoy your snack with your tea. The snack is usually welcomed because some consider Persian-style tea strong and bitter.

MAKING TEA PERSIAN STYLE

As stated, a samovar can be found in most homes in Iran. It is kept running from first thing in the morning until after dinner. Some Iranians who have relocated to the United States either didn't bring their samovars with them or found them cumbersome to use. If you don't own a samovar, you can still prepare tea the Persian way by using a teakettle to keep the tea warm.

Only loose-leaf tea is used, and I find the flavor to be most similar to black, Ceylon Earl Grey tea. Plan to use two teaspoons of tea leaves per person. Place the loose-leaf tea right into the teapot without a filter. Pour boiling water over the leaves and steep for ten to twenty minutes. When is the tea ready? My Persian friend Mahvash Ghoochan answered that question this way, "It is ready when you can smell it, and it smells strong because that is what makes the tea taste good." The tea is then poured into cups made of glass. Mahvash's favorite teacup is made of glass and has a handle called an *estekan*. A saucer is placed underneath the cup to protect the table from the heat. The guest is usually asked how they prefer their tea—strong or weak—and then just enough tea is poured into the cup, allowing room for the addition of hot water to match their personal taste. If the occasion is a bit more formal, all the teacups would be served from a tray.

To replicate a samovar, prepare the tea in a teapot as instructed and set aside. Next, heat water until it boils in a teakettle with a handle that can be tilted down and out of the way. Then take the lid off the teakettle and place the teapot on top of it. Keep the teakettle on the stove over low heat. This keeps the infusion warm and also provides a supply of warm water to dilute the brew to each guest's personal taste.

Iranian tea is served with very hard, white sugar cubes. My husband and I love Persian food, and a favorite lunch date for us is to meet at a local Persian restaurant. When I was first served tea in a Persian restaurant, I noticed that the sugar cubes were hard and didn't dissolve in my tea. I thought the cubes were old. I have since learned that sugar cubes can be made in varying degrees of hardness, depending on different countries' preferences. I also discovered that sugar cubes are sometimes made with sugar beets—not just the sugar cane I had grown used to seeing in Florida fields.

The Iranians and Russians are not only similar in the way they brew their tea, they also have latched on to the same way to sweeten their tea. Because both cultures seem to like their tea brewed long and strong, to some palates the tea tastes somewhat bitter. Sugar or something sweet is often needed to balance the taste. The hard sugar cubes are held between the front teeth as the tea is sipped through the sugar cube. If the sugar cubes were like the American kind, they would dissolve with the first sip. I can't seem to embrace this way of sweetening my tea, so I try to crush the cube in my tea and allow time for it to dissolve. I think my dentist might think this was a good idea too!

CULTURAL TIP:

Tarof is a way of showing modesty, dignity, and restraint in a back and forth gesture between two parties...and is demonstrated by always refusing to eat something when first asked.

TEATIME IN IRAN

Iranians start off each day with tea at breakfast time. They also have tea after lunch and dinner but usually not with the meal. It can also be consumed at an afternoon break with snacks such as dates, nuts, cookies, candies, or chocolate. Tea is always served hot.

Meals can be served at a table or, especially when there is a large crowd, on the floor. If on the floor, a tablecloth called a *sofreh* is spread over a beautiful Persian rug. Large platters of food are placed on top of the tablecloth, and everyone gathers around and sits cross-legged.

For a simple way to have tea Persian style, just serve it in the afternoon with some of the snacks mentioned previously. For the more adventurous, try making *sohan asali* and serving it alongside the other snacks. I think it tastes similar to a nut brittle.

All recipes in this chapter come from my Iranian friend Mahvash Ghoochan. Not only did she provide the recipes, but she also prepared all the dishes and graciously served them to me in her home—all this with generous servings of tea!

41

RECIPES

Flat Bread with Accompaniments

1 loaf flat bread (buy flat bread at a Persian or Middle Eastern
  store or use pita bread)
walnut halves
radishes, sliced in quarters
large basil leaves, washed and dried
1 bunch mint leaves, washed and dried
feta cheese

Place all the ingredients except flat bread in a bowl or on a
platter. When serving, pass the flat bread along with the bowl
or platter filled with accompaniments. It is customary to place
a small amount of each item from the bowl in the center of a
piece of flat bread before rolling up the bread and eating it.
This is a delicious way to begin a great Persian meal.

Sohan Asali

1 cup sugar
4 tablespoons butter
3 tablespoons honey
1 cup slivered almonds, washed, drained, and dried
⅓ teaspoon saffron—dissolve saffron in 1 tablespoon boiling
  water and set aside for 5 to 10 minutes

In a medium size saucepan, combine sugar, butter, and
honey. Heat on medium-high heat stirring occasionally until
the mixture turns to a medium golden color and the sugar
is completely dissolved (about 5 to 10 minutes). Add the
almonds and stir until the mixture becomes a darker golden
color. Add the dissolved saffron liquid and stir one or two more
times. Spoon the mixture into small dollops on a parchment-
lined cookie sheet. Allow to cool. Store in an airtight container.

Saffron Chicken

If you want a real treat, prepare this dish for lunch or dinner.
Finish the meal with tea and dessert.

*1 whole chicken fryer, cut into pieces (cut each breast in half
  to make all the chicken pieces about equal in size)*
vegetable oil
salt
*½ teaspoon saffron—dissolve saffron in ⅓ cup boiling water
  and set aside for 5 to 10 minutes*

Coat the bottom of a large frying pan with vegetable oil. Remove skin and fat from chicken pieces. Heat the frying pan on burner set to high. Place the chicken pieces in the hot oil and sprinkle with salt. Cook on high heat until the chicken begins to sizzle and turn a slight golden color. Reduce the heat to low, cover the pan, and continue cooking chicken for about 45 minutes to an hour or until done. Pour the saffron mixture into the frying pan, turning the chicken to coat well. Allow to cook 5 to 10 more minutes.

Rice

Rice is a staple for a Persian household. There are many recipes for different kinds of rice. Basmati rice is the most commonly used, and I like using the kind from India. This rice requires rinsing.

3 cups white basmati rice
1 tablespoon salt
6 cups water
5 tablespoons oil
5 tablespoons butter cut into tablespoons

Rinse the rice thoroughly 3 times in warm water and drain. Put rice, salt, and water in a large saucepan. Bring to a boil over high heat and then reduce to medium heat and allow to simmer about 20 minutes uncovered. Stir occasionally. Add the butter and oil to the top of the rice and reduce heat to low. Place a clean cloth or a couple paper towels over the pan and cover with a tightly fitting lid. Cook 40 minutes on low heat. Remove from heat and allow to cool for 5 to 10 minutes before serving.

Barberry Rice

This is a nice addition to rice, and it is one of my favorites. Barberries*, a tangy fruit similar to a cranberry, can be purchased in a Persian store or online. If necessary, dried cranberries can be substituted for the barberries. If cranberries are used, leave out the sugar.

2½ cups dried barberries
oil
3 tablespoons sugar
½ teaspoon saffron, dissolve saffron in
⅓ cup boiling water and set aside for
5 to 10 minutes

Soak barberries in cold water for one hour and then rinse. Put a small amount of oil into a medium size frying pan. Add the barberries, sugar, and saffron mixture. Bring to a boil, stir, and then turn off. Stir cooked rice into the barberry mixture and serve on a large platter or in a large bowl.

Baklava Cake

1 cup sugar
3 eggs
1 cup vegetable oil
3 tablespoons rose water*
1 tablespoon ground cardamom
1 cup almond meal or powder
1 teaspoon baking powder
2 cups all-purpose flour
2 teaspoons pistachios, finely chopped

Simple Syrup (for top of baked cake)
½ cup water
1 cup sugar
½ cup rose water

Preheat oven to 350 degrees. Beat eggs and sugar together until light and creamy. Add the vegetable oil and rose water and beat until combined. Add cardamom, almond meal or powder, baking powder, and flour and mix well. Pour into a greased 6 x 9 glass baking pan and bake for 20 to 25 minutes or until cake is set. While cake is baking, prepare the simple syrup by boiling the water and sugar together until sugar is completely dissolved. Add rose water and boil one more minute. Allow syrup to cool for a few minutes. Slice baked cake in small diamond shaped pieces, sprinkle with pistachios, and then spoon syrup evenly over the top. Allow cake to cool completely. Serve with tea.

France

Paris is called the "City of Lights," but it could also be called the "City for Tea Lovers." This large city in France is said to boast more than 150 "*salons de thé*," which simply translates to "tea salons." This is a statistic that even London is unable to compete with. A quote from the movie *Sabrina* sums it up. The character Sabrina Fairchild, played by Audrey Hepburn, says, "Paris is always a good idea." Indeed, it is definitely a good idea for people who are passionate about tea.

Although France would not necessarily be called a tea-drinking nation, the volume of tea the French consume is growing. England has always been associated with this beverage, but France was actually introduced to tea in 1636—that's about 22 years before tea reached England's shores. Tea was imported from the Dutch, and it soon became very popular, especially among the French aristocrats.

TEA PAST

Some of the earliest tales of tea drinking in France date from 1665. Following orders from his doctor, King Louis XIV was said to drink tea on a regular basis in hopes of curing his gout. He also believed that it was good for the heart because the Chinese and Japanese consumed large amounts of tea and didn't suffer from heart problems. Tea was commonly sold in apothecary shops and viewed more as a medicine than a delightful beverage. French doctors worked to publish many articles claiming tea's health benefits.

Madame de Sévigné was a popular member of the salon and court in Paris. She wrote many letters to her daughter, some of which detailed the tea-drinking practices of the rich and famous of her day. Madame made sure to tell her daughter about how Princess de Tarente drank more than 12 cups of tea a day. She would also point out in her gossip writings how another Frenchwoman named Marquise de la Sablière added milk to her tea. To make special mention of this fact obviously meant that this was something new to the madam. The trend to add milk to tea never really caught on with the French. It did, however, cross the English Channel—the British enjoy milk with their tea still today.

France stopped importing tea from the Dutch and started importing it directly from China around 1700. Tea continued to grow more popular with the upper class and was viewed as a drink for the rich. Coffee and chocolate were also growing in popularity but didn't seem to have the same self-indulgent and decadent ties as tea. While coffee and chocolate's popularity remained steady, tea's extravagant reputation led to its demise for a period of time. The impoverished people began to despise all things that represented the wealthy class, and tea was one of them. This unrest between the rich and poor brought on the French Revolution, a war between the classes in the late 1700s. As the bourgeois class gained victory, King Louis XVI and Queen Marie Antoinette were kicked out—and so was tea!

The French soon forgot about the problems associated with the tea and "all things English" became the trend, which started in the 1830s and 1840s. Sipping tea after dinner with dessert and as an afternoon snack with sweet goodies became fashionable in England. Not to be outdone, the French followed suit and quickly forgot about their aversion to tea.

The term *le five-o'clock* is now synonymous with teatime in France. However, some of the Brits did not consider imitation to be the best form of flattery. The *Pall Mall Gazette*, a British newspaper, published an article in December of 1885 that did not speak kindly of their neighboring country's teatime. It said, "There is something really touching in the strenuous effort of our French neighbors to imitate our afternoon tea as they term it, the 'five o'clock'… This is somewhat different from our afternoon tea, but our friends across the channel are happy and 'where ignorance is bliss, 'tis folly to be wise."

At about this same time, the French city of Limoges was producing some of the finest porcelain in the world. Limoges became the generic name synonymous with the beautiful porcelain made in that city. Serving tea with beautiful Limoges teapots and teacups at the tables of the upper class in France in the 19th century was a common sight. Today Limoges porcelain is considered collectable, and some pieces can be quite expensive.

Not worried about tea's comings and goings, two brothers opened up a tea import business, Mariage Frères*, in France in 1854. For generations before them, family members had been trading tea, spices, and other goods. Learning the family business under the tutelage of their father, Aimé Mariage, Henri and Edouard considered tea to be a good investment. Although the company had been in the family for nearly 130 years, in 1983 Mariage Frères was sold to someone outside of the family. However, to this day the business continues to operate from the original building in Paris' Marais district. They now sell their teas retail and have opened three tea salons in Paris, one of which has a tea museum in it. Here they serve their tea and tea-infused foods in the style they call the "French Art of Tea."

Tea has inspired artists who have visited and lived in France over the years. One of them was an American named Mary Cassatt. She spent quite a bit of time in France studying art and painting. In her later years, Mary called the country her home. Most of Mary's paintings reflect women doing what she thought to be ordinary things of the day. One of my favorites is a painting of two women drinking tea—it is named *Le Thé*, which simply means "the tea." This work of art, which was painted around 1880, now hangs in The Museum of Fine Arts in Boston.

In November of 1910, an article about the French tea craze appeared in the *New York Times*. In it was a quote from the Paris newspaper *Le Figaro* stating, "The entire social life of the city (Paris) revolves around a teapot." The author goes on to tell how the craze has spread beyond Paris. "Everywhere he finds people drinking tea—not quietly and in private but actually gulping it down in regular tea houses where there's 'standing room only.' " Paris tearooms have increased in number throughout the years. Tea might not be considered France's number one drink—they have so many wonderful beverages—but it definitely has a special place in the hearts of the French.

CULTURAL TIP: When meeting friends for tea, or anything else, it's customary to give a quick kiss on both cheeks.

Tea Present

Anthelme Brillat-Savarin, a French gourmet, lawyer, and author of *The Physiology of Taste*, describes what many people think about afternoon tea. He states, "Another novelty is the tea-party, an extraordinary meal in that, being offered to persons that have already dined well, it supposes neither appetite nor thirst, and has no object but distraction, no basis but delicate enjoyment."

In France today, tea may be a wonderful afternoon snack or perhaps enjoyed after dinner with dessert. Others who are true tea lovers may start their day with a cup as an accompaniment to breakfast or brunch. Although tea might not be taken at five o'clock as mentioned, teatime is still a favorite pastime of many, whatever the time of day.

Rachel Braussen, who lives just an hour and a half outside of Paris in Lorraine, explained to me that tea is still considered a "girl thing" despite the fact that the number of men from certain social classes who partake in tea is increasing. Typically the men from each village would meet, smoke, and drink coffee and alcohol in a *café* while the women, sometimes with their children, would meet in the quiet, smoke-free *salon de thè* where wonderful pastries were served. Rachel went on to tell me how she and her friends have tea together. She described it as a time to get together, usually between 2:00 and 4:00 in the afternoon and their children are at school or whenever they can sneak some time away.

Rachel loves to take a walk in the woods around her home with her friends. When done, they reward themselves with teatime. Afternoon tea in France is different than in England where scones, finger sandwiches, and desserts are served alongside the tea. In France, it isn't such an elaborate spread, but it is still full of flavor. The French are known for their skillfully made *patisserie,* which not only means "desserts" such as pastries and cakes but also refers to the bakery that sells them. A scrumptious *patisserie* and a delicious cup of tea are all that are needed for *le five-o'clock.*

Rachel has a great gift-giving idea, especially for a bridal shower or wedding gift. She loves to give a French tea with romantic names such as *Éros* or Wedding Imperial. Along with the tea, she includes a CD with the song "La Vie en Rose" by Edith Piaf. "La Vie en Rose" is considered by some to be the most famous romantic love song of all time. If your budget is a bit larger, you could include the French white porcelain teapot with its unique stainless steel cozy from Mariage Frères or the Plisse teapot made by Pillivuyt, which is featured on the cover. A copy of this book or any book on taking tea would be another lovely addition to the gift for a bride or bride-to-be. Be sure to look in the resources guide at the back of the book to find out where to purchase all of the French tea things!

MAKING TEA FRENCH STYLE

Just as the culinary and wine-making world has taken its craft to an art form in France, tea is no different. Mariage Frères, the oldest tea company in the country, has been significant in setting the standard of excellence regarding the making of tea, and their "French Art of Tea" has influenced the way tea is made. The same careful attention to detail that is so important in the culinary world is also necessary to make tea.

The "art" starts with choosing which tea to drink. It could be said that of all the people in the world, the French drink the widest variety of tea. This might be because they did not develop any tea traditions of their own that defined what was considered "proper." They are free to enjoy a variety of teas—from a light muscatel-tasting Darjeeling to a smoky Lapsang Souchong—based on their own preferences. Most tend to drink their tea *nature*, without sugar or milk added. When sugar is added, it is usually with the rough-cut natural sugar cubes.

Loose-leaf tea is considered the best tea of choice. Using the same terms and concepts as the wine industry, France has fabulous French-blend teas available but also offers great single-estate teas, and estate-blend teas. Appreciation is growing for teas from a specific region of a tea-growing country such as Darjeeling in India or even more specifically teas from a single estate within a region.

The "Art of Tea" continues with attention paid to how it is prepared. A keen sense of awareness and thought goes into the preparation.

- Proper measuring—measure one teaspoon loose-leaf tea for each cup of hot water. Place the tea leaves into a filter that is large enough to allow the leaves to expand.
- Good filtered water and correct water temperature—heat fresh water to 160 to 180 degrees Fahrenheit for green and white teas; 190 to 200 degrees for oolong; a full boil for black, herbal tisanes, fruit blends, and puerh.
- Infusing times—steep green and white tea leaves for 1 to 3 minutes; steep black, oolong, and puerh teas for 3 to 5 minutes; steep herbal tisanes and fruit blends for 5 to 10 minutes.
- Decanting and removing the tea leaves—promptly removing the tea leaves after properly steeping is essential to the art of tea!

TEATIME IN FRANCE

The presentation is the last step to this "art." The presentation doesn't need be fancy, but it should look as though time and effort were put into it. To get started, use a simple white porcelain teapot and matching cups, saucers, and plates. Next add crisply ironed cotton napkins and a tablecloth. If you own demitasse spoons, use them—they are very French! If you don't have any, use matching teaspoons and forks. Fresh flowers are always a nice touch for the table. Serve one of the following recipes with your favorite French tea. If you don't have time to bake, purchase a lovely *patisserie* from a local bakery or a quiche from your favorite specialty market. To make it really simple, just buy a few truffles from a decadent chocolate shop and *bon appétit*!

RECIPES

Spinach and Mushroom Quiche

This recipe has been created by my friend and colleague Chef Jae Gruber, who is an accomplished chef and instructor at Le Cordon Bleu College of Culinary Arts in Atlanta. Serve this dish for breakfast, brunch, lunch, or even a light dinner. Add some of the following pastry dishes for a delightful teatime.

4 eggs
¼ cup mayonnaise
2 tablespoons whole milk
1 teaspoon Dijon mustard
2 tablespoons all-purpose flour
4 tablespoons canola oil
½ cup yellow onion, diced
1 cup button mushrooms, sliced
1 garlic clove, minced
1 10-ounce package chopped frozen spinach, thawed, drained, and liquid squeezed out
¾ cup Swiss or Emmenthaler cheese, grated
2 teaspoons kosher salt
1 teaspoon black pepper, freshly ground
1 9-inch unbaked piecrust (may substitute ready-made refrigerated or frozen piecrust)

Preheat oven to 375 degrees. In a large bowl, whisk together eggs, mayonnaise, milk, mustard, and flour until thoroughly combined. Refrigerate while preparing other ingredients. Set a medium-sized sauté pan on a burner turned on to medium-high heat. When the pan is hot, add 2 tablespoons canola oil to the pan and watch for the "waves" in the oil, which means that the oil is hot. Add the mushrooms to the pan. Sauté until the mushrooms begin to caramelize and turn brown. Reduce heat to medium and continue to cook mushrooms for 5 minutes. Transfer the mushrooms to a small bowl. Return the pan to the burner and turn the heat on to high. Add the remaining 2 tablespoons of canola oil. Heat the oil, and then add the yellow onions. Sauté the onions on high heat, stirring for 2 minutes. Reduce heat to low. Continue cooking the onions for approximately 10 minutes, allowing them to slowly caramelize. Add garlic and allow to cook about 2 minutes. When done, cool slightly. Remove the quiche mix from the refrigerator and add the drained spinach, mushrooms, cheese, salt, and pepper. Stir to combine. Add slightly cooled onions and stir well.

Piecrust

1⅓ cups all-purpose flour
½ teaspoon kosher salt
½ cup cold vegetable shortening
3 to 4 tablespoons ice water

Prepare the piecrust by mixing flour and salt in mixing bowl. Cut shortening into the flour with a pastry cutter until the mixture resembles small peas. (Do not use your hands because the heat from your hands will cause the shortening to melt, which affects the flakiness of the crust.) Gradually add 3 teaspoons ice water while mixing with a fork. If it appears that the mixture needs more water, add one more tablespoon. To make the dough using a food processor, place the flour and salt into the bowl of the food processor fitted with a steel blade and pulse a few times to mix. Add the shortening and pulse 8 to 12 times or until the mixture resembles small peas. While using the pulse button, pour ice water through the feed tube one tablespoon at a time. Start with the first 3 tablespoons, and then add the last tablespoon if necessary to form dough. Transfer dough to a floured board. Work quickly to gather the dough into a ball. Wrap in plastic and refrigerate for 30 minutes. Remove the dough from the refrigerator. Using a floured rolling pin and floured board, roll from the center to the edge, turning and flouring the dough to make sure it doesn't stick to the board. When large enough to fit the pie pan, transfer the dough to the pie pan by carefully rolling it around the rolling pin or folding it into quarters.

Pour the quiche mixture into the uncooked deep-dish piecrust (homemade or frozen purchased variety). Place the quiche on a cookie sheet and then into the preheated oven. Cook for one hour, rotating the quiche halfway through the cooking time (30 minutes). Remove from oven and allow the quiche to stand for 15 minutes before serving. Slice with a serrated knife. Makes 8 luncheon-sized servings or 6 dinner-sized servings.

Orange Madeleines

These small shell-shaped sponge cakes are perfect for teatime. You will need a madeleine pan, which can be purchased at any kitchen store, to bake them.

1¼ cups all-purpose flour
½ teaspoon baking powder
¼ teaspoon salt
3 eggs
1 teaspoon vanilla extract
⅔ cup sugar
4 teaspoons orange zest
¾ cup salted butter, melted and cooled
2 tablespoons butter, melted (to grease the molds)
powdered sugar

Preheat oven to 350 degrees. Brush madeleine pan with melted butter. Combine flour, baking powder, and ¼ teaspoon salt in a bowl and set aside. In another bowl, beat the eggs until light yellow. Add vanilla extract. Slowly add the sugar. Continue beating until the volume has increased to about 4 times the original size. Gently fold in the orange zest and then the flour mixture. Stir in the melted and cooled butter. Spoon about 1 tablespoon of batter into each shell, filling the mold about ¾ of the way full. Bake 10 to 12 minutes or until tops are golden brown. Remove madeleines from the mold and place on a cooking sheet. Dust powdered sugar over the tops. Makes about 3 dozen.

Quatre Quart

This pastry recipe and the one following are from Rachel Braussen of France. They are her favorite teatime recipes. *Quatre Quart* is the French version of a pound cake. The name literally means four quarters—each of the four ingredients is of equal weight (see the list of ingredients). This simple recipe is very popular in Bretagne, or Brittany, in the western region of France.

3 extra large eggs (this usually weighs about 250 grams)
1⅓ cups sugar (250 grams)
1¼ cups salted butter (250 grams)
2½ cups all-purpose flour (250 grams)
1 tablespoon lemon juice (optional)

Preheat oven to 350 degrees. Beat sugar and butter together well. Separate egg whites from the yolks, placing the whites into one bowl and the yolks into another. Lightly beat the yolks. Add yolks to the butter and sugar and mix well. Add lemon juice if desired. Add flour and mix well. Beat egg whites until stiff. Gently fold one quarter of the egg whites into the batter with a spoon and then fold the rest of the egg whites in gently. Pour into a large greased cake or loaf pan and bake for 45 minutes or until toothpick swipes clean. Makes 6 servings.

Apple Tart

This recipe is Rachel's grandmother's recipe and is great served with tea.

Tart
⅔ cup all-purpose flour
⅓ cup butter, chilled
2 tablespoons sugar
1 egg yolk, beaten
pinch of salt

Apple topping
3 granny smith apples
2 tablespoons butter, cut into small pieces
3 tablespoons white sugar

Preheat the oven to 400 degrees. Sift flour into a large mixing bowl and set aside. Cut the butter into small pieces and use a pastry cutter to cut the butter into the flour until it looks like breadcrumbs (may use a food processor). Add the sugar. Mix in the beaten egg yolk and add warm water by the drop until the dough forms a ball. Chill the dough in the refrigerator for 30 minutes. Peel the apples. Cut them into quarters, remove the cores, and slice each section into four slices. Remove dough from the refrigerator. Sprinkle flour onto a cutting board or large piece of parchment paper and roll the chilled dough into a big circle about 1-inch thick. Line a greased 8-inch tart pan with the pastry. Prick it with a fork and trim the edges. If the dough has gotten too warm, refrigerate it. Arrange apple slices into circles on top of the pastry, sprinkle with sugar, and dot with butter. Bake for 30 minutes. Allow to cool, slice, and serve.

Morocco

Morocco is a country that is located in the northwest corner of Africa and is slightly larger than the state of California. On a clear day, you can see Spain from her Mediterranean coast.

Beginning approximately 2000 years ago with its first inhabitants, the Berber nomads, Morocco has been a home to many, and each group has left their own indelible mark. Conquerors from Phoenicia, Carthage, and Rome came and added to Morocco's melting pot of culture and cuisine. Having possibly the strongest and longest lasting influence on the people, the Arabs arrived and invaded Morocco during the seventh century. During the Middle Ages, Spanish and Jewish immigrants settled in the area. Even later, the French arrived and left their influence—evident in the number of patisseries along modern city streets.

Because the tea ceremony is performed all over the country—publicly in cafes and by street vendors and privately in homes—you might think the tea tradition has always been a part of the culture. That however, is not the case.

Tea Past

Though there are many varying accounts as to exactly when tea first came to Morocco, most experts concur that tea arrived sometime in the 1700s but was extremely limited. During that period, European diplomats brought gifts of tea to the king.

Noufissa Kessar Raji, author of *The Art of Tea in Morocco*, reportedly claims that Queen Anne of England (1644-1714) sent two great copper fountains and a little high quality tea to the court of Moulay Ismail (1672-1727). This information is quoted in an article within a Moroccan culinary magazine named *Saveur et Cuisine du Maroc*. According to the article, Raji states that Queen Anne was using tea to soften the heart of the Sultan who was holding 69 English prisoners of war. She apparently had some success because Raji goes on to say, "Throughout the 18th century, tea regularly accompanied English, Dutch, and Scandinavian diplomatic missions."

Yet others dispute those dates and make note that the first tea to reach the country was given as a gift to the Sultan of Morocco in 1720 from King George I of England. In the film *The Meaning of Tea*, Abedlahad Sebti, author of the book *From Tea to Atay*, indicates tea did not arrive in Morocco until the late 1700s. Regardless of when it arrived the first time, tea was really only consumed in certain regions and only by the privileged until the mid 1800s.

In the nineteenth century, trading ships delivered an unplanned supply of tea and started the phenomenon that is now deeply embedded in the Moroccan culture. When the British were unable to deliver their tea from China to the Baltic ports during the Crimean War in 1854, Morocco truly became a tea-drinking nation. Due to the embargoes, English ships had to find new ports to deliver their tea. The tea landed and was unloaded at the trading posts of Tangier and Mogador along Morocco's Atlantic coast.

In Morocco, it was very common to drink herbal infusions. The most popular was a mint tisane called *na'na* that grew in the country, especially in the mountain regions. The newly imported Chinese gunpowder tea known as *chun mee* was added to the sweet mint tisane. This blend soon became Morocco's national drink—enjoyed by people at all levels of society and throughout all regions of the country. They took the Chinese tea and basically invented a tea ritual and ceremony to call their

own. That unintentional British tea shipment started a national favorite pastime that seems to be here to stay.

Tea Present

If you have tasted Southern-style sweet tea and think it is sweet, you had better brace yourself for a cup of Moroccan-style tea. Made up of green gunpowder tea, mint, and sugar, it could surely be considered dessert. For the people of Morocco, that is sometimes the case.

To Moroccans tea is not only a beverage; tea is a way of life. It is part of their rules of hospitality and considered a family necessity. Moroccans value family time, and their homes are the places where they love to entertain. Tea and food are daily rituals that connect them to family members, friends, and strangers. Tea is the first thing a guest is offered upon entering someone's home. To refuse a glass of the mint tea, *atay bil na'na*, or at least a bite or two of the food being offered would be considered extremely rude. Furthermore, one glass of tea will not suffice—an obligatory three cups should be drunk. There is a saying in Morocco about the three cups of tea. The first cup is as bitter as life, the second is as strong as love, and the third is as soothing as death.

Tea is served with breakfast, which usually consists of some sort of fresh bread or French pastry such as a baguette, croissant, or Moroccan bread. Tea is served for a mid-morning snack at about 11:00 and also after lunch, which is the biggest meal of the day. Tea is served in the afternoon or early evening along with a small snack of pastries similar to an afternoon tea. Tea is served after dinner and sometimes with a dessert. It is enjoyed as a drink for pleasure and also used to aid digestion.

My good friend Darie Estill was amazed at the hospitality Moroccans offer strangers. While she was visiting the country, she and her group were invited into a stranger's home to share a meal with the family. She said that they all sat on pillows around a low table. Even though she didn't speak the same language as her host, she felt welcomed as they helped her group try to figure out how to eat the food they offered.

Darie also explained that everywhere you go, tea is being served—at street-side stands, restaurants, teahouses, which are called cafés, and private homes. The smell of tea permeates the air as you walk through the medina (old quarters) of any town or city. Merchants offer tea in their stores, often serving tea as they bargain or seal a deal.

Many have pondered how and why tea has almost overnight become such an important tradition in the hearts of the Moroccan people. Because alcohol is frowned upon for religious reasons and water purity is often questionable, tea, which is readily available in stores across the country and requires boiled water, is a practical beverage. The taste and smell of tea gives the tea drinker a sense of physical pleasure and relaxation. The tea's caffeine is a great pick-me-up, and the mint not only tastes good but also aids digestion—especially appreciated when enjoying some of the traditional, spicy foods.

No matter how busy Moroccans are or how much work is left to do, they always find time to gather with family and friends for a cup of tea and some good food. Drinking tea is never taken "to go." Taking time to sit and relax with others is essential.

CULTURAL TIP:

To refuse a glass of the mint tea, *atay bil na'na*, or at least a bite or two of the food being offered would be considered extremely rude. Furthermore, one glass of tea will not suffice—an obligatory three cups should be drunk. There is a saying in Morocco about the three cups of tea. The first cup is as bitter as life, the second is as strong as love, and the third is as soothing as death.

Making Tea Moroccan Style

Berber whiskey, as it is jokingly called, is another name for tea made Moroccan style. This style of tea has taken on its own ceremony and art form in Morocco.

Although it is not difficult to make, you do need a few essentials. A round silver or brass tray is nice to place all your items on. The teapot, or *barrad* as they call it in Arabic, is usually made out of silver-plate, aluminum, or stainless steel. Similar to a British "Manchester" in shape, it has a rounded body, a domed lid, and a long curved spout, which is perfect for pouring from great heights, as is the custom. You will also need Moroccan tea glasses. These heat resistant, colorful glasses usually have ornate gilding and rich patterns adorning their surfaces.

The ingredients needed to make the tea are very specific. Moroccans like to use Chinese gunpowder tea. You will also need fresh mint. In Morocco the mint chosen is a very specific varietal from the spearmint family, but regular spearmint will do just fine. Sugar is the last ingredient needed. Moroccans use hardened sugar cubes shaped in very long rectangles or a sugar cone, which is about eight inches long and wrapped in a purple paper. The sugar is broken off the cone with a copper hammer in just the right amount. These cones are readily available in Morocco and are given as gifts at dinner parties and weddings. Because sugar cones are hard to find in the United States, using regular granulated white sugar is fine but be prepared to have enough on hand because Moroccans like their tea sweet! Sometimes, depending on the region, lemon verbena, saffron, orange blossoms, and other spices are added for additional flavor.

The tea ceremony starts with heating water in a kettle. When the water boils, pour some into the teapot to warm it up a bit and then pour that out. Next, add the tea—approximately one teaspoon per cup of hot water—to the warmed teapot. Add boiling water from

the kettle, quickly rinse the tea leaves by swirling the teapot around, and discard the water. Then add a large bunch of fresh mint to the teapot, filling it about three-quarters of the way full. Add sugar. Moroccans use from 3 to 5 teaspoons of sugar per cup, but you may add sugar to suit your taste. Pour boiling water over the tea and mint and allow to steep about 3 to 5 minutes. Sometimes Moroccans will put their teapot right back on the stove and allow the water to come to a boil again, but this is not necessary.

After the tea has steeped, you are ready to pour the tea. This is where the art really comes in. The Moroccans like to aerate the tea and create froth on the top by pouring it back and forth two or three times between the teapot and the glass from high above. Although this may take practice, Moroccans consider this process important because it infuses the flavors of the tea and makes the tea taste better. Once the flavors have infused, the tea is ready to be served.

Practice pouring the tea from increasingly larger distances between the teapot and the glasses, doing your best not to spill. The experts can pour the tea from three or four feet into the glasses, but this kind of skill probably takes some time to acquire. (Author's note: I like to brew green tea with water that is below the boiling temperature because I think the flavor is better. I also prefer much less sugar than the Moroccans. I would add no more than two teaspoons sugar per cup of tea.)

TEATIME IN MOROCCO

Mealtime in Morocco involves a few interesting customs.

- Moroccans prefer to wash their hands before eating. For this purpose, sometimes a bowl of rose water or orange flower water* and towels are offered to guests before the meal is served. Otherwise towels soaked in the scented water are passed to guests. This is a nice touch—one you might consider doing.

- Moroccans prefer to eat with their hands. Traditionally they eat with their right hand, being careful to use only their first two fingers. Using more than two fingers is considered gluttonous. The left hand is used for picking up bread or passing food to other people. You might like to try this. However, be warned that it is an art form to eat couscous with your hands!

Because tea is served all day long, a Moroccan tea party can happen at any time of day. If you would like to have a breakfast tea, you could serve croissants or fresh baguettes with the tea. If you would like to have an afternoon tea, you could serve cookies made from the recipe listed or, even easier, buy already-made pastries and enjoy the afternoon. If you are interested in a lunch or dinner tea, prepare and serve the following recipes, which Darie Estill provided. After returning from her trip to Morocco, she quickly went to her kitchen and recreated her Moroccan experience at home.

$\mathcal{R}$ECIPES

Shlada Bil Litchine Wa Tamra (Orange and Date Salad)

This dish can be served as an appetizer or dessert. If used as a dessert, sprinkle with cinnamon. Sometimes a simple orange salad is served, using oranges and cinnamon alone.

6 sweet oranges, peeled and sectioned with juice from
    peelings squeezed over the sections
2 teaspoons orange flower water (may substitute with
    3 teaspoons orange zest or orange liqueur)
8 dried dates, pitted and thinly sliced lengthwise
¾ cup slivered almonds, lightly toasted
Mint leaves for garnish

Place oranges and juice in a bowl. Add orange flower water and stir gently to combine. Cover with plastic wrap and refrigerate. When thoroughly chilled, place the orange segments and juice in a large bowl and scatter the dates and almonds over the top. Sprinkle with mint leaves. Serve chilled. Makes 4 to 6 servings.

Hummus

1 16-ounce can chick peas, liquid reserved
juice of 1 lemon
1 or 2 cloves garlic
¼ cup olive oil
3 tablespoons tahini (sesame seed paste)
¼ teaspoon salt
ground pepper
paprika

Combine all ingredients except paprika in a food processor or blender and process until well-blended. If too thick and not fluffy, add reserved chick pea liquid a little at a time until desired consistency. Garnish with paprika and drizzle with additional olive oil. Serve with warmed pita bread or other flat bread. May also be served with vegetables or as a spread for sandwiches.

Harira

Traditionally Harira is used to break the fast of Ramadan. When Darie was in Morocco, she ate it at every restaurant that served it. The tang of lemon adds a bright note to the rich, thick soup.

¼ cup olive oil
¼ cup butter
1 large onion, chopped
2 stalks celery, chopped
1 cup lentils (I used red lentils)
½ cup fresh parsley, chopped
½ cup fresh cilantro, chopped (optional)
2 32-ounce cartons chicken broth
1 28-ounce can whole tomatoes
¼ cup tomato paste
1 can chickpeas
1 teaspoon white pepper
½ teaspoon cumin
1 teaspoon paprika
1 teaspoon turmeric
½ teaspoon ground ginger
2 teaspoons salt (or more to taste)
½ cup vermicelli, broken into half-inch pieces
1 egg, beaten
juice from ½ lemon
1 lemon quartered

Sauté onions and celery in butter and olive oil just until soft. Add next 7 ingredients and spices. When adding tomatoes, crush them with your hands and drop into the soup. Bring soup to a boil and then simmer for 45 minutes. Bring back to a boil and add the vermicelli pieces, allowing time to return to a simmer. Combine egg and lemon juice and stir into soup with a long spoon. Adjust seasoning to taste and simmer for 10 more minutes. The soup should be thick and rich. Serve with lemon wedges.

Couscous Chicken (or Lamb)

Couscous is traditionally prepared by steaming it so that each grain can swell slowly without sticking to the other grains. It is typically steamed over an aromatic stew, using a couscousiere. When dining at a restaurant in Morocco, let them know the day before or the morning of your arrival, so they can have the couscous prepared. Today very good instant couscous is available and ready to eat 5 minutes after adding boiling water to it. Though not necessary, the cooked couscous may be placed into a steamer or colander and set over this chicken stew to absorb the stew's aroma.

2 tablespoons olive oil
4 pounds chicken breasts with bone and skins or one 4-pound
    chicken cut into pieces (if lamb is preferred, use 2 pounds
    lean lamb shoulder meat without bone and 2 pounds lean
    lamb necks with bone)
1½ pounds or 5 cups quartered onions
3 quarts water
¼ cup honey
½ teaspoon saffron
2 teaspoons powdered ginger
1 teaspoon white pepper
3 teaspoons salt (or more to taste)
1 stick cinnamon
1 teaspoon ground cumin
½ teaspoon turmeric
¾ cup chopped dates or ½ cup golden raisins
6 carrots, cut into 2-inch lengths
4 medium yellow squash, quartered and cut into 2-inch lengths
5 medium zucchini, quartered and cut into 2-inch lengths
1 16-ounce can chickpeas, drained
2 20-ounce boxes 5-minute couscous
¼ cup butter
Tabasco or other hot sauce

In a large pot, sauté meat in olive oil over medium heat. Add 1 cup onions, stirring and shaking pot occasionally. Sauté about

5 minutes without browning. Add remaining onions, honey, and spices and cover the pot. Bring to a boil. Let simmer for 1 hour. Remove chicken with tongs and pull meat from bones. Return meat to the pot. Add dates or raisins, carrots, squash, zucchini, and chickpeas. Return to a boil and simmer for 30 to 60 minutes, skimming as needed. Add remaining onions, honey, spices, and water and cover the pot. Adjust seasoning to taste. Prepare couscous according to directions, adding salt to taste. Serve stew over couscous with a generous amount of butter and Tabasco if desired.

Ghoriba (Semolina Cookies)

1 cup plus 2 tablespoons unsalted butter
1¼ cups all-purpose flour
1 cup confectioners' sugar
2 cups semolina flour
2 eggs, beaten
1 teaspoon vanilla extract
1 egg white, lightly beaten
¼ cup blanched or slivered almonds

To make clarified butter, melt the butter in a saucepan over low heat. Skim off the froth and then pour into a mixing bowl, leaving the white mild solids in the pan. Set aside until cool. Sift the flour and confectioners' sugar into a bowl, add the semolina and a pinch of salt, and mix thoroughly. When the butter is cool but still liquid, stir in the eggs and vanilla. Then add the dry ingredients, mixing to a firm dough. Knead well, then cover the bowl with plastic wrap and leave for 1 hour. Line two cookie sheets with parchment or a silicone baking mat. Preheat oven to 350 degrees. Knead the dough again until smooth and pliable. Take 3 teaspoons of dough and shape into a smooth ball, then shape remaining dough into balls of the same size. Place on cookie sheets 1 inch apart (they do not spread). Brush the tops with egg white and press an almond on top of each cookie, which will also help flatten the cookie. Bake for 20 minutes or until lightly golden in color. Cool on cookie sheets. Makes about 50.

United States of America

In America, we were consumers of tea long before we were established as an independent nation. Many Americans view tea as an English drink, but we were actually sipping tea before it was ever imported to English soil. In 1650, trading ships brought tea to the Dutch colony of New Amsterdam, which is now known as New York City. England didn't receive shipments until around 1657.

TEA PAST

The American love affair with tea has not always been an approved indulgence. There was a time in our history that drinking tea was looked upon as unpatriotic. Although we never disliked the flavor, we opposed what tea came to represent—taxation without representation.

When most people think of America's tea party, they think of the Boston Tea Party. This "party" was actually a revolt where colonial citizens disguised as Mohawk Indians threw tea chests into the Boston harbor to protest what they felt were unfair taxes. What you may not realize is the Boston Tea Party was not the only revolt of this kind—several portside cities held their own rebellious "tea parties." Rebellion to the Tea Act took place in Charleston, South Carolina; Greenwich, New Jersey; New York City, New York; Philadelphia, Pennsylvania; and Annapolis and Chestertown, Maryland.

Charleston, South Carolina, then known as Charles Town, was actually the first town to show its opposition to taxation without representation. On December 8, 1773, the upset citizens prevented the ship named *The London* from unloading its 257 chests of tea for two weeks. After hearing whispers about citizens plotting to steal the tea

from the ship, British officers had the tea removed early one morning before it could be seized. They locked it up and stored it in the Exchange and Customs Building* for almost three years! Not to be outdone by Boston, about one year later, Charleston also had its own ceremonial "tossing of the tea into the sea" when another ship tried to unload tea there.

When South Carolina declared its independence in October 1776, the state sold the tea that had been locked up in the exchange building for quite a price to the tea-starved citizens. The proceeds went to help fund the Revolution. South Carolina not only profited from the tea rebellion, the state tossed it, consumed it, and a little later decided to grow it.

The South Carolina connection to tea continued as tea plants, known as the Camellia Sinensis, were brought to the state in about 1800 by André Michaux, the Royal Botanist to King Louis XVI of France. Along with other floral beauties, the Camellia Sinensis was planted for ornamental purposes at the Middleton Barony Plantation, now known as Middleton Place Plantation and Gardens*.

During the mid 1800s, tea farms were attempted

in several areas around South Carolina. In 1888, Dr. Charles Shepard started the Pinehurst Tea Plantation in Summerville with some degree of success. The tea grown there was said to be of good quality—their oolong tea won first place at the 1904 St. Louis World's Fair. Pinehurst thrived until Shepard's death in 1915.

Sir Thomas Lipton got involved in the tea industry in 1956. He leased the land where the Pinehurst Tea Plantation had once stood and later bought property on Wadmalaw Island, just south of Charleston, to continue his experimental project. Lipton brought cuttings of plants from the Middleton Plantation (the first American location to import and cultivate tea plants), the Pinehurst Tea Plantation, India, and China to start the farm. That land is now home to the Charleston Tea Plantation*, owned and operated by Bigalow Tea Company and Bill Hall.

In 1904, long before television and the Internet ever existed, the World Fairs were the primary places to learn about the latest research and most up-to-date information along with new technologies, recent inventions, and current trends. Visitors came from all over the world to see the latest innovations. In turn, they took what they learned back to their hometowns.

Pinehurst Tea Plantation's oolong award was not the only significant tea event at the 1904 St. Louis World's Fair. Because most Americans drank imported green tea from China and Japan up until this time, fairgoers were all abuzz about the iced tea samples being given out at the East Indian Pavilion. Although some give credit to Richard Blechynden, India's tea commissioner and director, for inventing iced tea, clear accounts of it being served prior to this are recorded. The earliest report of iced tea being served dates back to an 1879 cookbook called *Housekeeping in Old Virginia* in which iced tea was added to a "tea punch."

At the fair, however, Blechynden popularized the beverage. Recognizing that the summer heat was causing the hot and thirsty patrons to pass by the samples of the newly imported hot black Indian tea he was trying to market, Blechynden decided to try a different tact. The enterprising commissioner filled several large bottles with his tea and then turned them upside down to flow through iced lead pipes. Other reports state that he simply added ice to the brew. The cold iced tea was greatly appreciated by the parched fairgoers and helped to freely advertise his black Indian tea. Richard Blechynden forever changed the way most thought about consuming tea. Instead of drinking mostly hot Chinese and Japanese green tea, they began drinking mostly iced Indian black tea! Although most Americans continue to choose black tea to make their iced tea, the country from which the tea comes is not necessarily India—many new sources of tea have been discovered.

In addition to the iced tea, other American culinary icons were also being offered at the 1904 fair. Although the data is inconclusive as to where and when the invention of the hot dog on a bun, hamburger on a bun, and ice cream in a cone took place, no doubt the fair helped these favorite American foods grow popular. In a sense, they were the fast foods of the time. Everything could be bought and eaten as you walked. As fairgoers returned home, they took these culinary delights with them, and the rest, as they say, is history!

TEA PRESENT

American's love affair with tea has been growing in recent years. With more of us consuming tea on a daily basis, we drink an estimated 55 billion servings of tea a year. That equates to more than two and a half billion gallons of tea, and the numbers are growing. Not surprisingly, most of that, about 85 percent, is iced tea.

States are recognizing that tea is an American icon. South Carolina, whose tea relationship dates back to the birth of our country, passed a state bill in 1995 recognizing tea as their state's "Official Hospitality Beverage."

On April first in 2003, several Georgia state representatives proposed what started out as a humorous bill, but some Southerners took it very seriously. The bill in essence stated that any food service establishment that serves iced tea must serve sweet tea. The service establishment may serve unsweetened tea if they choose, but sweet tea is a requirement. It also stated that any person who violates this code section shall be guilty of a misdemeanor of a high and aggravated nature!

Having lived in the South most of my adult life, I must confess that I haven't been to a restaurant that did not offer sweet tea. In fact, while I was attending a national tea conference (yes, they do have these), I met a man who was quite high up in a nationally recognized tea company. When we were introduced, he thanked me. I wasn't quite sure what he meant, so I asked him why he thanked me. He said that he noticed my name tag indicated I was from Georgia, and that because of me and my neighboring states in the South, he was able to put all his kids through college because of our large consumption of tea!

When I visited Charleston a while back, I toured the Exchange and Customs Building. During the tour, we went to the lower level where the tyrannous tea had once been stored. The conditions were hot and humid, and I cannot imagine the stored tea tasting very good. The deprived tea lovers were probably desperate for their "cuppa."

Next I journeyed to the place where the tea plantations

once stood and toured Wadmalaw Island's tea fields. The Pinehurst Tea Plantation is now an established country club neighborhood with street names that reflect its rich heritage—Pekoe Court, Lipton Street, Shepard Lane, and Tea Farm Road. Most of the homes were built at the end of the last century, but a few buildings are more than a hundred years old, left over from the heyday of the tea plantation. If you know what you are looking for, you can still see some rows of tea plants amidst the lush landscape surrounding the homes.

The only tea plantation in the continental United States, the Charleston Tea Plantation offers scenic tours. For those interested, a tour with explanations of how tea is made and a tour of the tea fields are also available. If you are lucky enough to go when the tea is being harvested, you can see the tea being processed for consumption in the factory and drink a glass of iced tea made from the leaves plucked that same day!

MAKING TEA AMERICAN STYLE

Making iced tea is simple. I prefer making my tea from loose-leaf tea because I think the flavor is better and the choices are numerous. If you want to go outside the box a bit, choose a tea that is not black.

To brew one gallon of gourmet iced tea with loose-leaf tea

1. Use spring water or fresh, cold water from the tap. Do not reuse water that has already boiled—the oxygen will have evaporated from it, and this affects the taste of the tea.

2. Measure ⅓ cup tea leaves. Place them directly into the teapot or use a tea infuser that's large enough to allow the leaves room to expand and steep properly. For teas or herbals that require a heaping teaspoon for one cup of tea, like Rooibos, use ⅔ cup leaves.

3. Heat the water until it reaches the correct temperature: generally 160 to 180 degrees Fahrenheit for green and white teas; 190 to 200 degrees for oolong; and a full boil for black teas, herbal infusions, and fruit blends. A six-cup teapot is a good size to use. Pour water over the leaves immediately and cover the teapot.

4. Steep the tea for the time instructed on the tea package: generally 3 to 5 minutes for black teas, 3 to 5 minutes for oolong; 1 to 3 minutes for green and white teas; and 5 to 10 minutes for herbal infusions and fruit blends. Steeping too long can cause the tea to taste bitter.

5. Immediately after steeping, remove the leaves by straining the loose tea leaves from the teapot as you pour the tea into a pitcher or by removing the tea infuser.

6. Transfer the tea to a pitcher and sweeten it if desired. Then add enough cold tap or filtered water to make one gallon.

TEATIME IN AMERICA

Iced tea has become an American tradition. To my knowledge, no other country prefers to drink their tea iced like the United States does. Most people don't think they are having a tea party when they are drinking this thirst-quenching beverage, but they are! A tea party can be a party of one or it can be a party of many—sip a relaxing cup of tea in solitude while taking a break from a busy day or sip tea with guests in your home or friends at a restaurant. Tea parties happen when one or more people sip tea! Now pair up a favorite iced tea with a great hamburger and finish the party with some ice cream, and you have all the makings of an American style tea party.

The 1904 St. Louis World's Fair is the inspiration for this all-American menu with some twenty-first century style added in. The team who worked so hard to make this book come alive collaborated and came up with all the recipes. Some are old family favorites, and some are new family favorites, and we sincerely hope they will soon become your family's favorites!

RECIPES

Basil Burgers with Goat Cheese

Lauren Rubinstein, photographer of the beautiful pictures featured throughout this book, provided this delicious recipe.

8 Kaiser rolls
2 tablespoons butter
2 pounds ground chuck or ground turkey
8 tablespoons goat cheese
3 red bell peppers, seeded and sliced in half
16 large basil leaves, julienned (cut into thin slices)
¼ cup basil, chopped
salt and pepper to taste

Place peppers in a plastic bag and add a small amount of olive oil. Shake the bag to coat the peppers with the oil and then grill them till charred on the outside, about 15 minutes. Allow the peppers to cool, then peel the skin and chop each half into thin pieces. Mix ground beef or turkey with the 1/4 cup of chopped basil, salt, and pepper. Divide the meat into 6 to 8 burgers, depending on the size you would like serve. Grill according to individual taste. Spread a small amount of butter on each cut side of the rolls and toast rolls in oven or directly on grill. When burgers are done, place 1 tablespoon goat cheese, 2 to 4 julienned basil leaves, and 2 to 3 pieces of roasted pepper on top of burgers. Place on toasted bun and enjoy!

Heirloom Tomato, Corn, and Basil Salad

Annette Joseph, the photo stylist who created the stunning food shots in *The World in Your Teacup*, provided this tasty recipe.

5 large heirloom tomatoes, cubed
1 large bunch of fresh basil, chiffonade (cut into thin slices)
4 cups corn, fresh or frozen (defrosted)
1 small red onion, chopped finely
¼ cup red wine vinegar
¼ cup extra virgin olive oil
1 Meyer lemon
½ teaspoon salt
1 cup feta cheese

In a large bowl, combine cubed tomatoes, corn, half the basil chiffonade, and onion. To make the dressing, combine vinegar, olive oil, juice of 1 lemon, and salt in a small bowl and mix well. Pour the dressing over the vegetables, toss gently, and top with feta and remaining basil chiffonade. Serve immediately. Makes 6 servings.

Homemade Ice Cream

My husband's grandfather was called Big Daddy. He was Big Daddy to 28 grandchildren, 42 great-grandchildren, and 12 great-great-grandchildren to date. All 9 of his children remember making ice cream during their early days—many with Big Daddy standing near—and have passed the tradition down to each new generation. Big Daddy was a man of the Great Depression. To make ice cream, he had to freeze his own ice and chop it up with an ice pick. Afterward, he was quick to have whoever was making the ice cream gather up the scattered salt so that he could use it again the next time he made ice cream. This recipe is in honor of Big Daddy!

6 eggs
2 cups sugar
4 cups whole milk
3 cups heavy whipping cream
2 tablespoons pure vanilla extract
1 teaspoon salt
Optional – ¼ pint of fresh fruit

Beat eggs, sugar, and salt together. Pour milk into a large pot and add egg mixture to it. Cook mixture, stirring constantly over low heat until it thickens like custard. This will take about 20-30 minutes. Remove from heat and cool in refrigerator. It is best to allow it to cool completely overnight. Add cream and vanilla into cooled mixture and then pour it into an ice cream freezer and follow the directions for your freezer. Serve in cones or bowls and enjoy. Big Daddy often liked to add chopped fresh fruit for additional flavor.

Lisa's Homemade Hot Fudge

If you choose to serve your homemade ice cream in bowls, try my (Lisa Boalt Richardson) hot fudge recipe—it's a hit at our house! I often double the recipe and freeze half for a future ice cream party. I also cook up a batch, pour it into jars, and give the jars as gifts or as party favors for teatime guests.

1 12-ounce bag semisweet chocolate chips
½ cup butter
1½ cups sugar
1 12-ounce can evaporated milk
½ teaspoon salt
1 teaspoon vanilla

In a large heavy saucepan, melt chocolate chips and butter together over low heat. Add the sugar and salt and stir well. Gradually stir in the evaporated milk. Bring the mixture to a boil and then reduce to medium/low heat. Boil the mixture gently, stirring constantly for about 8 minutes. Remove from heat and add the vanilla. Serve warm over ice cream.

Bibliography

Batmanglij, Najmieh Khalili. *New Food of Life: Ancient Persian and Modern Iranian Cooking and Ceremonies*. Mage Publishers, 2008.

Goodbody, Joan. *Celebrating South Carolina Flavor: The Rich History of Palmetto Tea Production*. Carologue, 1993.

Hangar, Catherine. *World Food Morocco*. Lonely Planet Publications, 2000.

Hoyt, Scott Chamberlin. *The Meaning of Tea*. Tea Dragon Films, 2008.

Mallos, Tess. *The Food of Morocco*. Bay Books, 2008.

Mariage Freres. *Mariage Freres: The French Art of Tea*. Mariage Freres, 1997.

Miller, Ruth M. and Andrus, Ann Taylor. *Charleston's Old Exchange Building: A Witness to American History*. History Press, 2005.

Mitchell, Evelyn. *Kiambethu: The First Tea Farm in Kenya*. Kiambethu Farm and Solutions for Business, 1994.

Pettigrew, Jane. *Tea in the City: Paris*. Benjamin Press, 2007.

Pettigrew, Jane. *The New Tea Companion*. National Trust Enterprises, 2005.

Pettigrew, Jane. *The Social History of Tea*. National Trust Enterprises, 2001.

Pratt, James Norwood. *New Tea Lover's Treasury*. Publishing Technology Associates, 1999.

"Tea in Morocco: An Amber Coloured Nectar," *Saveurs et Cuisine du Maroc*. www.saveursetcuisinedumaroc.com/en/index.php?option=com_content&task=view&id=5&Itemid=5.

Tsioulcas, Anastasia. *Traditional Tastes of Morocco*. September, 2005.

Other Resources

Specialty Tea Institute Certification Program: Level I, II, III. www.teausa.org.

The Tea Association of the United States. www.teausa.org.

The United Kingdom Tea Council. www.tea.co.uk.

Resource Guide

China

www.theteahouse.com—*Yixing* teapot, *gongfu* tea ceremony supplies (waterproof tray or tray with drainage holes, thimble teacups), *gaiwan* brewing vessels, tea, tea ware, and an educational DVD on *gongfu* tea ceremony by Dan Robertson

England

www.theteahouse.com—"Brown Betty" English teapot

www.janepettigrew.com—English tea specialist, historian, writer, consultant, and a friend in tea

www.vintagetea.com—paper filters, tea infusers

www.teaandetiquette.org—Tea and Etiquette® Masterclass and materials

www.tealeavesandthyme.com—Kim Jordy, owner of this wonderful tearoom in Woodstock, Georgia, supplied some of the English recipes listed in this book

www.tasteofbritain.com—Banger sausages (although the sausages are not listed on the website, they are available to order—with overnight shipping—by calling the number listed at the bottom of the home page) and many things English

Kenya

Kiambethu Farm, PO Box 41, 00217 Limuru, Kenya; Telephone: 066 73084/73419

www.magicalkenya.com—information about Kenya

Russia

www.ekaterinas.com—Russian porcelain, samovars, "Cobalt Net" tea set featured in photos

Iran

www.kalamala.com—online source for barberries and rose water

France

www.mariagefreres.com—Mariage Frères' official website

www.theculturedcup.com—Dallas, Texas tea store that stocks French tea, including Mariage Frères and the French porcelain featured on the cover

Morocco

www.thespicehouse.com—orange flower water

www.saharaimport.com—Moroccan import store in Berkeley, California that stocks many of the tea ware featured in photos

United States of America

www.oldexchange.com—British tea was seized and stored in the Old Exchange Building in Charleston, South Carolina

www.middletonplace.org—The first tea plants planted in the United States were planted at Middleton Place Plantation and Gardens

www.bigelowtea.com/act—Charleston Tea Plantation

Tea Tours

www.teawithfriends.com—tours of New York City Tearooms, including some specializing in foreign cultures

www.theteahouse.com—tours of countries of origin: India, Nepal, Ceylon, China, Japan, Korea.

Tea and Tea Ware

www.theteahouse.com

www.teasetc.com

www.theculturedcup.com

www.vintagetea.com

Ethnic Dinnerware, Glassware, and Accessories

www.worldmarket.com

www.anthropologie.com

www.pier1.com

www.bdjeffries.com

Cooking Gadgets, Table Linens, and Tea Accessories

www.cookswarehouse.com

www.southernseason.com

www.anthropologie.com

www.crateandbarrel.com

www.potterybarn.com

Craft and Paper Supplies

www.hobbylobby.com

www.michaels.com

Fabrics

www.forsythfabrics.com

www.designersguild.com

www.lsfabrics.com

Acknowledgments

It has been an honor to work with the Harvest House team on my second book. Thank you so much for believing in my book ideas. Everyone has been great to work with, and a big thank-you goes to Jean Christen and Peggy Wright, my editors.

I am so blessed to have such a great husband. His name should have been listed as coauthor because he spent so much time reading and editing the manuscript for this book. Thanks, Joe, for always being there.

My sister, Wendy McNeece, is not only a special sister but a great friend as well. Thanks for helping with edits!

A special thank-you goes to my daughter, Kate, for her help with kitchen cleanup and recipe testing. I appreciate you sacrificing your time for your mom.

This book is beautiful because a very talented and creative team helped make my words come alive. Thank you, Lauren, for your beautiful photos and your hard work on the photo shoot—you have a true gift! Annette, thanks for styling the book with such panache—you are truly talented!

Gracious Contributors

Special thanks go to all who contributed recipes and information (listed in the order of appearance within the book): Jean Christen (China); Dan Robertson, The Tea House (China); Beth Johnston, Teas Etc. (China); Lynayn Mielke, East West Tea Emporium (China); Jane Pettigrew (England); Kim Jordy, Tea Leaves and Thyme (England); David Walker, Walker Teas (Kenya); Yelena Shalansky (Russia); Mahvash Ghoochan (Iran); Rachel Braussen (France); Chef Jae Gruber, Le Cordon Bleu College of Culinary Arts, Atlanta (France); Darie Estill (Morocco); Annette Joseph (United States of America); Lauren Rubinstein (United States of America); the Smelser Family (United States of America).